APPLES

IN THE KITCHEN

APPLES
IN THE KITCHEN

90 DELICIOUS RECIPES USING APPLES, SHOWN IN
OVER 245 MOUTHWATERING PHOTOGRAPHS

EDITED BY FELICITY FORSTER

southwater

This edition is published by Southwater,
an imprint of Anness Publishing Ltd,
108 Great Russell Street,
London WC1B 3NA;
info@anness.com

www.southwaterbooks.com; www.annesspublishing.com

If you like the images in this book and would like to investigate
using them for publishing, promotions or advertising, please visit
our website www.practicalpictures.com for more information.

A CIP catalogue record for this book
is available from the British Library.

Publisher: Joanna Lorenz
Senior Editor: Felicity Forster
Photographers: Peter Anderson, Martin Brigdale, Nicki Dowey, Jake
    Eastham, Gus Filgate, Ian Garlick, Amanda Heywood, David Jordan,
    Dave King, William Lingwood, Charlie Richards, Craig Robertson,
    Simon Smith, Sam Stowell, Debi Treloar and Jon Whitaker
Illustrator: Maj Jackson-Carter
Designer: Nigel Partridge
Production Controller: Pirong Wang

Previously published as part of a larger volume,
The Illustrated World Encyclopedia of Apples

PUBLISHER'S NOTE
Although the advice and information in this book are believed to be
accurate and true at the time of going to press, neither the authors nor
the publisher can accept any legal responsibility or liability for any errors
or omissions that may have been made nor for any inaccuracies nor for
any loss, harm or injury that comes about from following instructions
or advice in this book.

NOTES
Bracketed terms are intended for American readers.

For all recipes, quantities are given in both metric and imperial
measures and, where appropriate, in standard cups and spoons.
Follow one set of measures, but not a mixture, because they are
not interchangeable.

Standard spoon and cup measures are level. 1 tsp = 5ml,
1 tbsp = 15ml, 1 cup = 250ml/8fl oz.

Australian standard tablespoons are 20ml. Australian readers
should use 3 tsp in place of 1 tbsp for measuring small quantities.

American pints are 16fl oz/2 cups. American readers should use
20fl oz/2.5 cups in place of 1 pint when measuring liquids.

Electric oven temperatures in this book are for conventional ovens.
When using a fan oven, the temperature will probably need to be
reduced by about 10–20°C/20–40°F. Since ovens vary, you should
check with your manufacturer's instruction book for guidance.

The nutritional analysis given for each recipe is calculated per portion
(i.e. serving or item), unless otherwise stated. If the recipe gives a range,
such as Serves 4–6, then the nutritional analysis will be for the smaller
portion size, i.e. 6 servings. The analysis does not include optional
ingredients, such as salt added to taste.

Medium (US large) eggs are used unless otherwise stated.

Main front cover image shows Apple Strudel – for recipe, see page 69.

CONTENTS

INTRODUCTION

The apple has long been one of the most popular – if not the most popular – of all fruits and much time and energy have been devoted to its development. Prized for its taste and keeping qualities, the humble apple is now the most widely cultivated tree fruit, both in commerce and in gardens.

No one knows exactly when apples were first discovered and eaten, but they are believed to have originated in Turkey. The fruit would have been taken via ancient trade routes to virtually every part of the huge land mass that comprises Eurasia.

In more modern times, trees have been introduced into the Americas, southern Africa and Australasia. Nowadays they are grown throughout temperate parts of the globe and have become of great significance to the economies of many countries as an exportable commodity. Such is the adaptability of the apple, that it is only in tropical, desert and extremely cold regions that trees cannot be relied on to produce good crops.

Due to their ease of cultivation and their tolerance of changeable climates, apples have never been considered a luxury food. Historically, they were an essential element in the diet of many peoples from all strata of society.

A versatile fruit

Down the centuries, apples have been bred for improved size and flavour and, very importantly, for storing for use when fresh fruits and vegetables are in short supply. Not only are the fruits delicious eaten straight from the tree but, unlike many other fruits, they can be transported over long distances or kept for many months without any adverse effects on their flavour.

Besides the types that are grown for eating raw, the vast range of varieties – running into thousands – includes apples for cooking, for juicing and for cider making. In the kitchen, fruits can be used both for sweet and savoury dishes; the tart, acid flavour of some is a perfect complement to many rich or fatty meats, especially pork and game, while others have a flavour as sweet as strawberries or pineapples.

Above: The quintessential apple recipe – a deep-filled farmhouse apple pie. The apples, sugar, spices and flour create a thick and syrupy sauce inside the pie.

With today's international trade and improvements in storage, there is not a single day of the year when a tasty apple cannot be enjoyed. Walk into any supermarket and you will have a choice of several varieties. A farm shop or farmers' market, where locally produced foods are sold, may offer an even wider selection.

A fruit for health and fitness

'An apple a day keeps the doctor away' is an old proverb, and recent research suggests that there may well be more than a grain of truth in this. The fruit contains natural substances that studies indicate may be able to play a significant part in strengthening bones and lowering cholesterol, as well as providing some protection against certain cancers, Alzheimer's disease, asthma and other respiratory diseases. This is aside from their natural vitamin content and the dietary fibre they provide, both essential in a balanced diet.

Apples are also the ultimate convenience food – they are small enough to slip into a lunch box (or even your pocket), and they provide an ideal snack when you are on the move and hunger strikes.

In this book

This volume celebrates the versatility of the apple by bringing together a selection of 95 enticing recipes for appetizers, salads, side dishes, main courses, desserts, cakes, preserves and drinks. There is also an illustrated guide to popular apple varieties and the basic techniques needed for preparing and cooking them, from peeling and coring to poaching and caramelizing. Whether you'd like a healthy fruit juice, a traditional apple pie or an indulgent sweet strudel, you'll find a wealth of delicious ideas in these pages.

Right: Apples provide an excellent source of natural vitamins and dietary fibre – all essential components of a balanced diet.

APPLE VARIETIES

With more than 7,500 apple cultivars known to exist worldwide, it is not surprising that this well-loved fruit comes in such a diverse range of shapes and sizes. Here are a few popular apple varieties to choose from. When selecting, apply the smell test – a good apple will have a pleasing, lightly perfumed aroma.

Above: Blenheim Orange is red with fine russeting and a rich, nutty flavour. It has yellowish-white, fine-textured and rather dry flesh which cooks well to a purée.

Above: Bramley's Seedling has waxy-skinned, sometimes flattened, irregular, green fruits with an acid flavour. The flesh collapses on cooking.

Above: Cortland is bright greenish-yellow with an uneven deep red flush. The white flesh is moderately juicy and slightly coarse in texture, but with a sweet, refreshing flavour.

Above: Cox's Orange Pippin is yellowish-green with a red stripe and an orange flush. The creamy-white flesh is crisp and juicy, with an intensely aromatic flavour.

Above: Fuji has rounded fruits that are yellow-green with a pink-red flush and flecking. The dull white flesh is crisp and juicy, with a slightly subacid flavour.

Above: Golden Delicious has slightly conical, sometimes irregular fruits that are yellow. The creamy-white flesh is crisp and juicy, with a sweet, aromatic flavour.

Above: Granny Smith is bright green with lighter flecking. The creamy-white flesh is firm, rather coarse-textured and juicy, with a refreshing, subacid flavour.

Above: Howgate Wonder is bright greenish-yellow with a red flush and striping. The creamy-white flesh is firm, fine-textured, juicy and sweet, with an aromatic flavour.

Above: Jonathan has irregular fruits that are bright greenish-yellow with a strong bright red flush. The creamy-white flesh is soft, fine-textured, fairly juicy and sweet.

Above: Braeburn has attractively marked reddish fruits on a yellow to light green background. The flesh is pale cream to golden yellow, and has a spicy-sweet flavour with nutmeg and cinnamon hints.

Above: Mutsu has irregular fruits that are bright yellow-green with some russeting. The creamy-white flesh is firm, fine-textured and juicy with a slightly sweet, somewhat acid but refreshing flavour.

Above: McIntosh is bright green with a dark bluish-red flush and some striping and flecking. The white flesh is soft, fine-textured and juicy, with a sweet, vinous flavour.

Above: Newtown Pippin is bright green with some russeting and darker spotting. The creamy-white flesh is firm, fine-textured and juicy, with a trace of richness.

Above: Northern Spy is yellow-green with a strong dark red flush and some spotting. The yellow flesh is fairly firm, juicy and sweet, with a pleasant flavour.

Above: Pink Lady has slightly conical to oblong fruits that are yellow with a distinctive pinkish-orange flush. The creamy-white flesh is crisp, firm and very sweet.

Above: Royal Gala is green with a pinkish-red flush. The creamy-white flesh is firm, crisp, fine-textured and juicy, with a sweet and good aromatic flavour.

Above: Winesap has slightly irregular fruits that are dull yellow-green with a pinkish-red flush. The yellowish-white flesh is firm, tender and coarse, with a sweet, subacid flavour.

BASIC TECHNIQUES

Once you have chosen the variety of apple you wish to use, there are a few basic techniques that you need to know, whether you want to eat your apple raw, cook it whole or use it as an ingredient in a savoury or sweet recipe. These pages illustrate the most common techniques for storing and using apples in the kitchen.

Apples can be kept for varying lengths of time, depending on the variety. A few even seem to improve during storage, as this allows the flavour to develop fully. Fruits intended for storage must be unblemished. Ideally, they should be stored at a temperature of 0°C (32°F), to slow down further ripening. They should be individually wrapped so that they do not touch each other while being stored. Otherwise, any rot that develops in an individual fruit will be rapidly passed on to the others.

After washing or wiping with a damp cloth, apples can be peeled, cored and cut. Dessert apples can be eaten raw without peeling, but for cooking, peeling is often necessary. You should try to pare off the skin as thinly as possible to avoid losing the valuable nutrients under the skin.

After these preparations, apples can be cooked in an enormous variety of ways, such as poaching, stewing, puréeing, baking, microwaving, pan-frying, deep-frying, caramelizing and sautéeing. They can also be preserved by either drying or being bottled in alcohol.

Storing

Above: Use pieces of silicone paper or baking parchment, about 30cm (12in) square, or less if the apples are small. Place an apple in the centre of each piece. Wrap the paper evenly around the fruit, twisting it at the top to secure it.

Peeling

Above: Before peeling an apple, wash the fruit and then pat it dry using kitchen paper. Use a small, sharp paring knife or a vegetable peeler to thinly peel all round the fruit. If you do this carefully, you will end up with a spiral of apple peel.

Coring

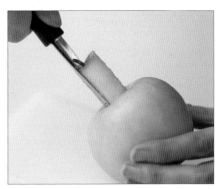

Above: Place the sharp edge of a corer over the stem end of the fruit. Press down firmly, then twist slightly; the core, complete with pips (seeds), will come away in the centre of the corer. Push out the core from the handle end.

Cutting

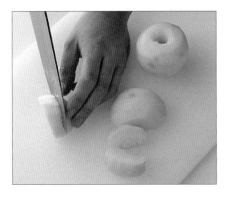

Above: Halve each apple, then cut each half into quarters or eighths. Depending on the size of the apple variety, cut each of the segments once more to produce 16 equally sized slices.

Poaching

Above: Poaching syrup consists of 1 part sugar boiled with 2 parts water for about 2 minutes. Bring this to the boil. Lower the heat and add cored, sliced apples. Simmer gently until the fruit is just tender.

Stewing

Above: Cut up the fruit. Put in a pan with just enough water, wine or fruit juice to cover. Add sugar to taste. Simmer gently until tender. Only stir if you want the apple to become a pulp.

Puréeing

Above: Mash cooked, peeled apples with a potato masher for a coarse purée. For a finer purée, whizz cooked, peeled fruit in a food processor or push through a food mill.

Baking

Above: Put apples in an ovenproof dish, add a little water, and sprinkle with sugar. Top with butter or stuff with sultanas. Bake at 180°C/350°F/Gas 4 until tender.

Microwaving

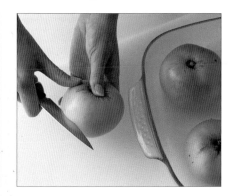

Above: Whole apples should be scored before microwaving, or they may burst. Place the fruit in a suitable dish, cover and cook on High until tender.

Pan-frying

Above: Peel and core apples and cut them into chunks or slices. Put a little butter in a pan on medium-high heat and add the apple pieces. Cook for about 5 minutes, stirring constantly, until the apple becomes golden brown and tender.

Deep-frying

Above: Peel and core the fruit. Heat oil for deep-frying to 185°C/360°F. Coat the apples in batter and deep-fry until the fritters rise to the surface and they are golden brown on both sides. Drain on kitchen paper and sprinkle with sugar.

Caramelizing

Above: Heat 50g/2oz/¼ cup butter and 50g/2oz demerara (raw) sugar in a heavy pan. Place cored and halved apples cut side down in the mixture and cook gently for 5 minutes. Turn the apples, cover, and then cook for a further 10–15 minutes.

Sautéeing

Above: Slice or dice cored apples (peeling them first is optional). Toss the pieces quickly in hot butter until they are lightly browned. Add sugar and flavourings, such as cinnamon or maple syrup, to taste.

Drying

Above: Peel, core and slice the apples. Lay the pieces on a baking sheet, cut side up. Dry in an oven that has been preheated to the lowest possible temperature. Cool completely before storing.

Preserving in alcohol

Above: Wash, dry and cut up the fruit. Place in a pan and cover with an equal weight of sugar. Leave for 1 hour. Tip into a jar and add rum to cover the fruit. Cover with clear film (plastic wrap) and store in a cool, dark place.

APPLE RECIPES

Apples come in a wide range of shapes, colours, flavours and textures so there's bound to be a fruit to suit your taste or need. Whether it's a tart, savoury appetizer or main course or an indulgently sweet dessert or after-dinner treat that you are after, the versatile apple is the perfect ingredient for so many tasty recipes. Some varieties such as Winesap or Bramley's Seedling are suitable for cooking with, while other crisp eating varieties such as Cortland or Granny Smith are ideal for juicing or eating raw grated in salads.

The apple recipes in this section are accompanied by clear, simple instructions. To start your meal, you could try a warming Curried Apple Soup or light Poached Apples with Berry Compote. There are a great variety of appley main dishes to choose from including Pumpkin and Apple Risotto, Spiced Pork Roast with Apple and Thyme Cream Sauce and Roast Goose with Apples, and delicious desserts range from Apple and Blackberry Crumble to Crunchy Apple and Almond Flan.

Above left: Apple fritters with fruit compote.
Above right: Apple-stuffed crêpes.
Left: Orchards provide the perfect shade for a picnic.

APPETIZERS, SALADS AND SIDES

The humble and inexpensive apple can be used to create all manner of mouth-watering hot or cold appetizers, salads and side dishes. From colourful and refreshing fruit soups to tart and tangy salads and accompaniments, this chapter highlights the apple's amazing versatility.

Apple and juniper soup

This is an excellent example of the delicious savoury fruit soups that are popular throughout northern Europe. The contrasting apple and juniper flavours in this recipe are particularly popular in Norway.

Serves 4
15ml/1 tbsp juniper berries
4 cardamom pods
3 whole allspice
1 small cinnamon stick
a bunch of fresh parsley
30ml/2 tbsp olive oil
3 cooking apples, peeled,
   cored and diced
2 celery sticks, finely chopped
2 shallots, chopped
2.5cm/1in piece fresh root ginger,
   finely chopped
1 litre/1¾ pints/4 cups light
   chicken stock
250ml/8fl oz/1 cup (hard) cider
250ml/8fl oz/1 cup double
   (heavy) cream
75ml/5 tbsp Armagnac (optional)
salt and ground black pepper
chopped fresh parsley, to garnish

1 Put the juniper berries, cardamom pods, allspice and cinnamon in a piece of muslin (cheesecloth) and tie together with string. Tie the parsley together.

2 Heat the oil in a pan, add the apples, celery, shallots and ginger, and season with salt and pepper. Place a piece of dampened baking parchment on top, cover the pan and cook gently for 10 minutes. Discard the parchment.

3 Add the stock and cider and stir well. Add the spices and parsley. Bring slowly to the boil, then lower the heat and simmer for 40 minutes. Remove the spices and parsley.

4 Pour the soup into a blender and blend until smooth, then sieve (strain) into a clean pan. Bring to the boil and add the cream and Armagnac, if using. Add salt and pepper if necessary. Serve hot, garnished with parsley.

Per portion Energy 406kcal/1677kJ; Protein 1.4g; Carbohydrate 8.5g, of which sugars 8.1g; Fat 39.2g, of which saturates 21.7g; Cholesterol 86mg; Calcium 48mg; Fibre 1.2g; Sodium 29mg.

Curried apple soup

Coconut milk replaces cream in this spicy soup for a smooth, rich texture.

Serves 4
50g/2oz/4 tbsp butter
2 shallots, finely chopped
1 cooking apple, peeled and chopped
10ml/2 tsp curry paste
30ml/2 tbsp plain (all-purpose) flour
1.25 litres/2¼ pints/5½ cups chicken stock
400ml/14fl oz can unsweetened
   coconut milk
salt and ground black pepper

To garnish
60ml/4 tbsp double (heavy) cream
chopped fresh parsley

1 Melt the butter in a pan, add the shallots and cook for about 5 minutes until soft. Add the apple and seasoning and cook for another 2 minutes.

2 Stir in the curry paste and flour and cook for 1–2 minutes. Remove from the heat and gradually stir in the stock. Return to the heat and, stirring all the time, cook until the sauce thickens. Simmer for 10 minutes.

3 Stir in the coconut milk and heat gently. Pour into bowls and garnish.

Per portion Energy 195kcal/812kJ; Protein 1.7g; Carbohydrate 14.3g, of which sugars 7.6g; Fat 15g, of which saturates 9.2g; Cholesterol 37mg; Calcium 66mg; Fibre 1.3g; Sodium 200mg.

Parsnip and apple soup

The Romans introduced apple orchards to England. Since then the country has been proud of its wonderful range of apples, and many fine apple juices are now available, often made from single varieties. For this soup, choose a fairly sharp-tasting juice – it will complement the sweetness of the parsnips and the warmth of the spices.

Serves 4–6
25g/1oz/2 tbsp butter
1 medium onion, finely chopped
1 garlic clove, finely chopped
500g/1¼lb parsnips, peeled and
    thinly sliced
5ml/1 tsp curry paste or powder
300ml/½ pint/1¼ cups apple juice
600ml/1 pint/2½ cups vegetable stock
300ml/½ pint/1¼ cups milk
salt and ground black pepper
thick natural (plain) yogurt, and chopped
    fresh herbs such as mint or parsley,
    to garnish

1 Melt the butter in a large pan and add the onion, garlic and parsnips. Cook gently, without browning, for about 10 minutes, stirring often to avoid sticking.

2 Add the curry paste or powder and cook, stirring, for 1 minute.

3 Add the juice and stock, bring to the boil, cover and simmer gently for about 20 minutes until the parsnips are soft.

4 Process or blend the mixture until smooth and return it to the pan.

5 Add the milk and season to taste with salt and pepper.

6 Reheat the soup gently and serve topped with a spoonful of yogurt and a sprinkling of herbs.

Per portion Energy 130kcal/548kJ; Protein 3.4g; Carbohydrate 18.5g, of which sugars 12.6g; Fat 5.3g, of which saturates 2.9g; Cholesterol 12mg; Calcium 101mg; Fibre 4g; Sodium 56mg.

Carrot and apple soup

Combining the sweetness of carrots with the fruity taste of apples creates a wonderful soup that you can enjoy all year round.

Serves 4
50g/2oz/¼ cup butter
1 onion, roughly chopped
1 garlic clove, roughly chopped
500g/1¼lb carrots, roughly chopped
1 large cooking apple, peeled, cored
    and roughly chopped
100ml/3½fl oz/scant ½ cup white wine
500ml/17fl oz/generous 2 cups
    vegetable stock
100ml/3½fl oz/scant ½ cup apple juice
salt and ground white pepper
200ml/7fl oz/scant 1 cup single
    (light) cream
100ml/3½fl oz/scant ½ cup crème fraîche
15ml/1 tbsp dry-fried pumpkin seeds
    and 5ml/1 tsp fresh chives, to garnish

1 Melt the butter in a pan. Add the onion and cook for 5 minutes until softened. Add the garlic and cook for a few minutes more. Stir in the carrots and the apple.

2 Add the wine, stock and apple juice. Season with salt and pepper. Bring to the boil, then simmer for 15 minutes. Add the cream and the crème fraîche and bring to the boil again.

3 Blend the soup with a hand blender. If it seems too thick, add some more stock. Serve with a sprinkling of pumpkin seeds and chopped chives.

Per portion Energy 341kcal/1412kJ; Protein 3g; Carbohydrate 18.2g, of which sugars 16.5g; Fat 27.2g, of which saturates 16.8g; Cholesterol 71mg; Calcium 84mg; Fibre 3.7g; Sodium 150mg.

Apple and cranberry soup

Fruit soups are mostly summer dishes, made with berries that are in season then. This tasty soup, however, is better suited to later in the year when cranberries are readily available, and it is perfect for festive meals around Christmas and New Year.

Serves 6
600g/1lb 6oz/5¼ cups cranberries
200ml/7fl oz/ scant 1 cup water
115g/4oz/generous ½ cup caster (superfine) sugar
350g/12oz cooking apples, peeled and finely grated
15ml/1 tbsp cornflour (cornstarch)
100ml/3½ fl oz/scant ½ cup sour cream

1 Put the cranberries in a large pan, add the water and bring to the boil. Simmer gently for 10 minutes, or until the cranberries are soft. Allow the cranberries to cool a little.

2 Transfer the cranberries and liquid to a food processor or blender and pulse to a purée. Pass the purée through a sieve (strainer), pressing down with the back of a spoon. Discard the fruit pulp and keep the strained fruit and juices. Add the sugar, put back in the pan and gently bring back to a simmer.

3 Add the grated apples to the cranberry mixture. Mix the cornflour with 30ml/2 tbsp water to make a smooth paste, then stir into the soup. Simmer, stirring, for 5 minutes. Allow the soup to cool, then transfer to a bowl and chill. Ladle the cold soup into bowls and add a dollop of sour cream to each serving. Swirl the sour cream with a skewer to decorate.

Per portion Energy 130kcal/552kJ; Protein 1.2g; Carbohydrate 25.1g, of which sugars 22.8g; Fat 3.5g, of which saturates 2.1g; Cholesterol 10mg; Calcium 35mg; Fibre 2.4g; Sodium 12mg.

Apple, kohlrabi and caraway soup

This chunky apple and kohlrabi soup is absolutely delicious, having a delightfully sweet edge.

Serves 4–6
10g/¼oz/½ tbsp butter
1 kohlrabi, diced
2 carrots, diced
2 celery sticks, diced
1 yellow (bell) pepper, seeded and diced
1 tomato, diced
1.5 litres/2½ pints/6¼ cups vegetable stock
800g/1¾lb crisp, tart eating apples, peeled
15ml/1 tbsp sugar
2.5ml/½ tsp ground caraway seeds
salt and ground black pepper
45ml/3 tbsp sour cream
a small bunch of parsley, leaves chopped

1 Put the butter in a large pan and melt over medium heat. Add the diced vegetables and sauté for 3–4 minutes, or until soft. Season to taste.

2 Add the vegetable stock and bring to the boil, then reduce the heat to low and simmer for 1 hour.

3 Grate the apples and add to the simmering soup, followed by the sugar and the caraway seeds. Cook for a further 15 minutes and adjust the seasoning.

4 Stir in the sour cream and sprinkle with the parsley to garnish. Serve hot.

Per portion Energy 104kcal/442kJ; Protein 1.6g; Carbohydrate 18.1g, of which sugars 17.9g; Fat 3.4g, of which saturates 1.9g; Cholesterol 8mg; Calcium 69mg; Fibre 4.6g; Sodium 44mg.

Apples with bacon

In this classic Danish open sandwich, the sweet combination of apples and onions mixed with crisp, salty bacon is both rich and satisfying. Apples appear in many savoury dishes in Denmark, from the classic pork loin stuffed with prunes and apples, to poached apple halves filled with currant jelly, served as a side dish with roast pork.

Serves 4
8 unsmoked streaky (fatty) bacon
  rashers (strips)
75g/3oz/1 cup finely chopped onion
2 firm apples, peeled and chopped
25g/1oz/2 tbsp salted butter, softened
2 slices rye bread
2 leaves round (butterhead) lettuce
4 parsley sprigs, to garnish

Cook's tip
Choosing crisp, tart eating apples for this recipe will give the best results.

1 Fry the bacon rashers over a medium-high heat until they crispen; drain the bacon on kitchen paper, leaving the fat in the pan.

2 Cook the finely chopped onion in the reserved bacon fat for about 5–7 minutes, until transparent but not browned.

3 Add the chopped apples, and continue cooking for a further 5 minutes, until tender.

4 Crumble half the bacon into the apple mixture.

5 Butter the slices of bread to the edges, top with the lettuce leaves and cut each slice in half. Leaving one curl of lettuce visible on each piece, spoon the apple and bacon mixture on to the lettuce, dividing it evenly among the sandwiches.

6 Break the four reserved bacon rashers in half, and place two pieces on each sandwich. Garnish with parsley sprigs, and serve warm.

Per portion Energy 215kcal/895kJ; Protein 9.8g; Carbohydrate 13.9g, of which sugars 8g; Fat 13.7g, of which saturates 6.4g; Cholesterol 40mg; Calcium 21mg; Fibre 2g; Sodium 883mg.

Black pudding with apple and potato

Black pudding has come a long way from its humble origins. Traditionally grilled or fried and served as part of a full English breakfast, black pudding now features on many a contemporary restaurant menu. Made in West Cork, Ireland, and widely available, Clonakilty black pudding is especially popular.

Serves 4

4 large potatoes, peeled
45ml/3 tbsp olive oil
8 slices black pudding (blood sausage), such as Clonakilty
115g/4oz cultivated mushrooms, such as oyster or shiitake
2 eating apples, peeled, cored and cut into wedges
15ml/1 tbsp sherry vinegar or wine vinegar
15g/1oz/2 tbsp butter
salt and ground black pepper

1 Grate the potatoes, putting them straight into a bowl of water as you grate them. Drain and squeeze out the excess moisture.

2 Heat 30ml/2 tbsp olive oil in a large non-stick frying pan, add the grated potatoes and season. Press the potatoes into the pan with your hands.

3 Cook the potatoes until browned, then turn over and cook the other side. Slide the cooked potatoes on to a warm plate.

4 Heat the remaining oil and sauté the black pudding and mushrooms together for a few minutes. Remove from the pan and keep warm.

5 Add the apple wedges to the frying pan and gently sauté to colour them golden brown. Add the sherry or wine vinegar to the apples, and boil up the juices. Add the butter, stir with a wooden spatula until it has melted and season to taste with salt and ground black pepper.

6 Cut the potato cake into wedges and divide among four warmed plates. Arrange the black pudding and cooked mushrooms on the bed of potato cake, pour over the apples and the warm juices and serve immediately.

> **Variation**
> If you are not keen on black pudding, you could try replacing it with mini burgers made from minced (ground) pork, or some sliced spicy sausages.

Per portion Energy 247kcal/1034kJ; Protein 4.2g; Carbohydrate 28.8g, of which sugars 5.4g; Fat 13.6g, of which saturates 4g; Cholesterol 13mg; Calcium 16mg; Fibre 2.4g; Sodium 132mg.

Beetroot, apple and potato salad

This attractive salad is from Finland, where it is served on Christmas Eve, just as the festive excitement mounts.

Serves 4
1 eating apple
3 cooked potatoes, finely diced
2 large gherkins, finely diced
3 cooked beetroot (beets), finely diced
3 cooked carrots, finely diced
1 onion, finely chopped
500ml/17fl oz/generous 2 cups double
 (heavy) cream
3 hard-boiled eggs, roughly chopped
15ml/1 tbsp chopped fresh parsley
salt and ground white pepper

1 Cut the apple into small dice. Put in a bowl and add the potatoes, gherkins, beetroot, carrots and onion and season with salt and pepper. Carefully mix together and spoon into individual serving glasses or bowls.

2 Mix any beetroot juice into the cream to flavour and give it a pinkish colour, then spoon over the vegetables and apple. Sprinkle the chopped eggs and parsley on top before serving.

> **Variation**
> Stir in ½ finely chopped salted herring fillet or 2 finely chopped anchovy fillets to the mixture with the parsley to add an extra dimension to the dish. Omit the added salt.

Per portion Energy 717kcal/2959kJ; Protein 8.5g; Carbohydrate 11g, of which sugars 10.2g; Fat 71.5g, of which saturates 42.9g; Cholesterol 314mg; Calcium 114mg; Fibre 2.3g; Sodium 132mg.

Beetroot and apple salad

These two typically English ingredients complement each other well to make a pretty salad, with the apple pieces turning pink on contact with the beetroot juices. The crispness of the apple contrasts well with the soft texture of the cooked beetroot.

Serves 4
6 beetroot (beets)
30ml/2 tbsp mayonnaise
30ml/2 tbsp thick natural (plain) yogurt
2 crisp eating apples
a small handful of chopped fresh chives
salt and ground black pepper
salad leaves and/or watercress sprigs,
 to serve

1 Wash the beetroot gently, without breaking their skins. Trim the stalks until very short but do not remove them completely. Put into a pan and cover well with water. Bring to the boil and simmer gently for 1–2 hours, depending on their size, or until soft throughout (check by inserting a sharp knife into the centre). Drain and leave to cool. When cold, remove the skins and cut into small cubes.

2 In a large bowl, stir together the mayonnaise and yogurt.

3 Peel the apples, remove their cores and cut into small cubes.

4 Add the beetroot, apples and two-thirds of the chives to the mayonnaise mixture and toss until well coated, seasoning to taste with salt and pepper. Leave to stand for 10–20 minutes.

5 Pile on to a serving dish. Add salad leaves and/or watercress sprigs and sprinkle with the remaining chives.

Per portion Energy 191kcal/793kJ; Protein 4.1g; Carbohydrate 9.5g, of which sugars 8.8g; Fat 15.5g, of which saturates 1.6g; Cholesterol 0mg; Calcium 54mg; Fibre 2.7g; Sodium 58mg.

Apple and leek salad

Fresh and tangy, this simple salad of sliced leeks and apples with a lemon and honey dressing can be served with a range of cold meats as part of a summer meal. For the best result, make sure you use slim young leeks and tart, crisp apples.

Serves 4
2 slim leeks, white part only,
 washed thoroughly
2 large eating apples
15ml/1 tbsp chopped fresh parsley
juice of 1 lemon
15ml/1 tbsp clear honey
salt and ground black pepper

1 Thinly slice the leeks. Peel and core the apples, then slice thinly.

2 Put in a large serving bowl and add the parsley, lemon juice, honey and seasoning to taste.

3 Toss well, then leave to stand in a cool place for about an hour, to allow the flavours to blend together.

Per portion Energy 59kcal/252kJ; Protein 1.9g; Carbohydrate 12.5g, of which sugars 11.8g; Fat 0.6g, of which saturates 0.1g; Cholesterol 0mg; Calcium 27mg; Fibre 3.4g; Sodium 4mg.

Sauerkraut salad with apple and cranberries

This sauerkraut salad is a Russian classic. Cabbage is a staple ingredient in Russia and the best soured cabbage can be bought in the market halls, where you are invited to taste both the cabbage and the brine. It is not unusual for a customer to taste up to ten different kinds before making a decision.

Serves 4–6
500g/1¼lb sauerkraut
2 red apples
100–200g/3¾–7oz/scant 1–1¾ cups
 fresh cranberries or lingonberries
30ml/2 tbsp sugar
60–75ml/4–5 tbsp sunflower oil
2–3 sprigs fresh parsley, to garnish

1 Put the sauerkraut in a colander and drain thoroughly. Taste, and if you find it is too sour, rinse it under cold running water then drain well.

2 Put the sauerkraut in a large bowl. Slice the apples or cut into wedges. Add the apples and the cranberries or lingonberries to the sauerkraut. Sprinkle over the sugar, pour the oil on top and mix all the ingredients well together.

3 To serve, turn the sauerkraut into a serving bowl and garnish with the parsley sprigs.

> **Cook's Tip**
> Cover the salad and chill for a few hours to allow the flavours to develop.

Per portion Energy 105kcal/437kJ; Protein 1.3g; Carbohydrate 8.8g, of which sugars 8.8g; Fat 7.4g, of which saturates 0.9g; Cholesterol 0mg; Calcium 49mg; Fibre 3.1g; Sodium 493mg.

Herring, ham, apple and beetroot salad

This colourful salad looks stunning and makes a perfect light snack.

Serves 4
2 fillets of pickled herring, drained and diced
1 large potato, boiled and diced
2 large cooked beetroot (beets), peeled and diced
1 small onion, grated
2 medium tart apples, cored and cut into thin wedges
2 gherkins, chopped
200g/7oz thick piece of ham, diced
2 thinly sliced hard-boiled eggs
salt and ground black pepper
30ml/2 tbsp finely chopped fresh dill, to garnish

For the dressing
100ml/3½fl oz/scant ½ cup sour cream
15ml/1 tbsp vinegar (any kind)
15ml/1 tbsp wholegrain mustard
1 medium beetroot (beet), finely grated
5ml/1 tsp creamed horseradish

Variation
Add a small amount of freshly grated horseradish root for a little extra heat.

1 To make the dressing, put the sour cream in a bowl and add the vinegar, mustard, grated beetroot and horseradish. Season to taste and combine well. Set aside.

2 Put the herring in a large bowl with the potato, beetroot, onion, apples, gherkins and ham. Season and mix together gently.

3 Add the dressing to the mixed salad and gently toss together to combine.

4 Transfer the salad to serving bowls, top each with the sliced hard-boiled eggs and garnish with dill, then serve.

Per portion Energy 355kcal/1495kJ; Protein 25g; Carbohydrate 30.8g, of which sugars 22.2g; Fat 15.4g, of which saturates 4.5g; Cholesterol 160mg; Calcium 84mg; Fibre 4.2g; Sodium 1169mg.

Carrot and apple salad

This refreshingly sweet and fragrant salad looks colourful and tastes good. Adding the lemon juice will help the grated carrot, apple and ginger to keep their natural brightness.

Serves 1
90g/3½oz carrots, peeled and coarsely grated
2 eating apples, coarsely grated
2.5cm/1in piece fresh root ginger, peeled and finely grated
juice of ½ lemon or 15ml/1 tbsp cider vinegar
5ml/1 tsp clear honey
a handful of alfalfa sprouts or other beansprouts
5ml/1 tsp sesame seeds, to garnish

1 In a large bowl, mix together the carrots, apples, ginger, lemon juice or cider vinegar and honey.

2 Place in a small bowl and press down, then turn out on to a plate to make a neat 'castle'. Top this with the alfalfa sprouts and sprinkle with sesame seeds to garnish.

Variation
Try replacing the apples with pears, and the carrots with grated courgette (zucchini). This cooling choice will give extra vitamin C.

Per portion Energy 194kcal/818kJ; Protein 3g; Carbohydrate 41g of which sugars 39g; Fat 3g of which saturates 0g; Cholesterol 0mg; Calcium 70mg; Fibre 6.6g; Sodium 36mg.

MAIN DISHES

Apples make a fantastically diverse contribution to numerous main courses and are often used in savoury cooking to add flavour and texture. A popular accompaniment to pork, apples also go surprisingly well with duck and game birds, as well as many fish and vegetarian dishes.

Pilaff stuffed apples

Vegetables and fruit stuffed with an aromatic pilaff are a great favourite in the summer months. This recipe is for stuffed apples, but you can easily use it to make an impressive medley of different stuffed fruit and vegetables for a buffet or a summer lunch.

Serves 4
4 cooking apples, or any firm,
   sour apple of your choice
30ml/2 tbsp olive oil
juice of ½ lemon
10ml/2 tsp sugar
salt and ground black pepper

For the filling
30ml/2 tbsp olive oil
a little butter
1 onion, finely chopped
2 garlic cloves
30ml/2 tbsp pine nuts
30ml/2 tbsp currants, soaked in
   warm water for 5–10 minutes
   and drained
5–10ml/1–2 tsp ground cinnamon
5–10ml/1–2 tsp ground allspice
5ml/1 tsp sugar
175g/6oz/scant 1 cup short grain rice,
   thoroughly rinsed and drained
1 bunch each of fresh flat leaf parsley
   and dill, finely chopped
1 lemon and a few fresh mint or basil
   leaves, to serve

1 Make the filling. Heat the oil and butter in a heavy pan, stir in the chopped onion and garlic and cook until they soften. Add the pine nuts and currants and cook until the nuts turn golden.

2 Stir in the spices, sugar and rice, and stir to combine thoroughly. Pour in enough water to cover the rice – roughly 1–2cm/½–¾in above the grains – and bring to the boil.

3 Taste, then season the mixture with salt and pepper to taste and stir to combine. Lower the heat and simmer for about 10–12 minutes, until almost all the water has been absorbed.

4 Toss in the chopped herbs, stir to combine and remove from the heat. Cover the pan with a dry, clean dish towel and the lid, and leave the rice to steam for 5 minutes.

5 Preheat the oven to 200°C/400°F/ Gas 6. Using a knife, cut the stalk ends off the apples and set them aside to use as lids.

6 Carefully core each apple, removing some of the flesh to create a cavity that is large enough to stuff.

7 Take spoonfuls of the rice and pack it into the apples. Replace the lids and stand the apples, upright and tightly packed, in a small baking dish.

8 In a jug (pitcher), mix together 100ml/3½fl oz/scant ½ cup water with the oil, lemon juice and sugar. Pour over and around the apples, then bake for 30–40 minutes, until the apples are tender and the juices are caramelized.

9 Serve the baked apples with lemon wedges and a sprinkling of mint or basil leaves to garnish.

Per portion Energy 382kcal/1595kJ; Protein 5g; Carbohydrate 54.1g, of which sugars 18.8g; Fat 16.5g, of which saturates 1.9g; Cholesterol 0mg; Calcium 26mg; Fibre 2.1g; Sodium 4mg.

Pumpkin and apple risotto

Pumpkin and other squash are very popular in the winter months. If pumpkins are out of season, use butternut or onion squash – the flavours will be slightly different, but they both work well.

Serves 3–4
225g/8oz pumpkin flesh or
   butternut squash
1 cooking apple
120ml/4fl oz/½ cup water
25g/1oz/2 tbsp butter
25ml/1½ tbsp olive oil
1 onion, finely chopped
1 garlic clove, crushed
275g/10oz/1½ cups risotto rice,
   such as Vialone Nano
175ml/6fl oz/¾ cup fruity white wine
900ml–1 litre/1½–1¾ pints/3¾–4 cups
   simmering vegetable stock
75g/3oz/1 cup freshly grated
   Parmesan cheese
salt and ground black pepper

1 Cut the pumpkin into small pieces. Peel, core and roughly chop the apple. Place the pumpkin and apple chunks in a pan and pour in the water. Bring to the boil, then simmer for about 15–20 minutes until the pumpkin is very tender. Drain, return the pumpkin mixture to the pan and add half the butter.

2 Mash the mixture roughly with a fork to break up any overly large pieces, but keep the mixture quite chunky. Heat the oil and remaining butter in a pan and fry the onion and garlic until the onion is soft.

3 Add the rice. Cook, stirring constantly, over a medium heat for 2 minutes until it is coated in oil and the grains are slightly translucent.

4 Add the wine and stir into the rice. When all the liquid has been absorbed, begin to add the stock one ladleful at a time, making sure each addition has been absorbed before adding the next ladleful. This should take approximately 20 minutes.

5 When roughly two ladlefuls of stock are left, add the pumpkin and apple mixture together with another addition of stock. Continue to cook, stirring well and adding the rest of the stock, until the risotto is very creamy.

6 Stir in the Parmesan cheese, adjust the seasoning and serve immediately.

Per portion Energy 439kcal/1831kJ; Protein 13.2g; Carbohydrate 59.1g, of which sugars 3.6g; Fat 13.3g, of which saturates 7.4g; Cholesterol 32mg; Calcium 264mg; Fibre 1.1g; Sodium 245mg.

Herring fillets in oatmeal with apples

Although traditionally herrings were eaten salted or smoked, herrings are now more likely to be eaten fresh. The tartness of the apple rings in this dish is a perfect accompaniment to the oily fish.

Serves 4
8 herring fillets
seasoned flour, for coating
1 egg, beaten
115g/4oz/1 cup fine pinhead
    oatmeal or oatflakes
vegetable oil, for frying
2 eating apples
25g/1oz/2 tbsp butter

1 Wash the fish and pat dry with kitchen paper. Check that all bones have been removed.

2 Toss the herring fillets in the seasoned flour, and then dip them in the beaten egg and coat them evenly with the oatmeal or oatflakes.

3 Heat a little oil in a heavy frying pan and fry the fillets, a few at a time, until golden brown. Drain on kitchen paper and keep warm.

4 Core the apples, but do not peel. Slice them thinly. In another pan, melt the butter and fry the apple slices until softened, then serve the herring fillets with the apple slices.

Per portion Energy 420kcal/1754kJ; Protein 26.5g; Carbohydrate 24.3g, of which sugars 3.4g; Fat 24.8g, of which saturates 7.6g; Cholesterol 120mg; Calcium 97mg; Fibre 2.6g; Sodium 209mg.

Smoked haddock with apple and vegetables

This light recipe is full of the fresh flavours of sautéed apples, leeks and root vegetables to complement the poached smoked haddock. Smoked cod could be used instead.

Serves 4

5ml/1 tsp caraway seeds
5ml/1 tsp butter
2 leeks, finely sliced lengthways
3–4 thin carrots, finely sliced
1 parsnip, finely sliced lengthways
2 cooking apples, peeled and sliced
   in wedges
250ml/8fl oz/1 cup vegetable stock
4 fillets smoked haddock, 250g/9oz
   each, bones removed
salt and ground black pepper
30ml/2 tbsp finely chopped fresh
   parsley, to garnish

Cook's Tip
A light horseradish cream is a delicious accompaniment to this dish.

1 Put the caraway seeds in a dry pan over a medium-high heat and toast them for 1 minute, or until they release their aroma. Heat the butter in a deep pan over a medium-high heat and add the leeks, carrots, parsnip and apples. Season to taste and add the caraway seeds. Turn the heat to medium and cook, stirring gently, for 3–5 minutes.

2 Add the stock and reduce the heat to low. Cook for 10–12 more minutes. Add the fish fillets to the stock, making sure that they are covered by the stock and vegetables. Cook for a further 5 minutes.

3 Remove the fish, using a slotted spoon, and arrange in a deep serving plate. Spoon over some of the cooked vegetables and cooking liquid. Sprinkle with the chopped parsley and serve.

Per portion Energy 323kcal/1368kJ; Protein 51.1g; Carbohydrate 21.8g, of which sugars 17.2g; Fat 4.1g, of which saturates 1.2g; Cholesterol 93mg; Calcium 152mg; Fibre 8.3g; Sodium 1947mg.

Haggis, potato and apple pie

Haggis is traditionally served with 'neeps and tatties' (mashed swede and mashed potatoes), but here is another way to serve your haggis, with just a little refinement and the extra sumptuousness of puff pastry. Apple combines very well with haggis as its tart and sweet taste cuts through the richness of the meat.

Serves 4
450g/1lb potatoes
1 garlic clove, crushed with 1 tsp salt
freshly grated nutmeg
400g/14oz ready-made puff pastry
300g/11oz haggis
2 cooking apples, peeled and cored
1 egg, beaten
salt and ground black pepper

1 Preheat the oven to 220°C/425°F/ Gas 7. Peel and slice the potatoes and mix with the crushed garlic. Season with a little freshly grated nutmeg and salt and ground black pepper.

2 Roll out the puff pastry into two discs, one about 25cm/10in in diameter and the other a little larger.

3 Place the smaller pastry disc on a baking tray and spread half the potatoes over it, leaving a rim of about 2cm/¾in all the way round.

4 Cut the haggis open and crumble the meat in a layer to cover the top of the sliced potatoes. Finely slice the apples into circles and spread all over the haggis. Then top the apples with the rest of the potatoes.

5 Brush the egg all around the exposed pastry rim, then place the other pastry circle on top, pushing down on the rim to seal. Use a fork to tidy up the edges and then press down around the edge again to create a firm seal. Leave to rest for 10 minutes.

6 Brush over with more egg and bake the pie in the preheated oven for 10 minutes to set the pastry. Then reduce the oven temperature to 200°C/400°F/ Gas 6 and bake for a further 40 minutes until evenly browned and cooked. Serve in slices with broccoli and mustard.

> **Variation**
> You could also use a tart variety of eating apple, such as Granny Smith.

Per portion Energy 698kcal/2919kJ; Protein 15.8g; Carbohydrate 72.9g, of which sugars 6.1g; Fat 41.2g, of which saturates 5.8g; Cholesterol 68mg; Calcium 88mg; Fibre 1.9g; Sodium 901mg.

German sausages with apple sauerkraut

These finger-length Bratwurst sausages taste delicious with sauerkraut and sourdough bread.

Serves 4
25g/1oz/2 tbsp butter
50g/2oz bacon, diced
1 onion, chopped
500g/1¼lb canned sauerkraut
3 allspice berries
3 bay leaves
2.5ml/½ tsp caraway seeds
200ml/7fl oz/scant 1 cup apple juice
1 apple, peeled, cored and diced
2 carrots, grated
5ml/1 tsp potato flour (potato starch)
30ml/2 tbsp vegetable oil
24 bratwurst sausages
salt, ground white pepper and sugar
chopped fresh parsley, to garnish
medium-hot mustard and sourdough
    bread, to serve

1 Heat the butter in a large pan over medium heat and gently fry the bacon and onion for about 3 minutes. Add the sauerkraut, the spices and the apple juice. Cook for 30 minutes, stirring occasionally and adding more apple juice if needed. Add the diced apple and grated carrots and cook for a further 5 minutes.

2 Blend the potato flour to a smooth paste with a little apple juice or water and stir it into the sauerkraut. As it comes back to the boil, the remaining juices will thicken and the sauerkraut will become shiny. Season to taste with salt, pepper and sugar, then spoon into a serving dish and keep warm.

3 Heat the oil in a frying pan over high heat, and fry the sausages for 6–10 minutes, turning frequently, until they are browned on all sides and cooked through. Arrange the sausages on top of the sauerkraut and garnish with chopped parsley. Serve with mustard and slices of sourdough bread.

Per portion Energy 644kcal/2675kJ; Protein 18.6g; Carbohydrate 34g, of which sugars 17.5g; Fat 49.1g, of which saturates 19.8g; Cholesterol 81mg; Calcium 159mg; Fibre 5.2g; Sodium 2207mg.

Braised sausages with onions, celeriac and apple

For this recipe, choose your favourite good-quality sausages, such as classic pork, Cumberland, duck or wild boar.

Serves 4
30ml/2 tbsp vegetable oil
8 meaty sausages
2 onions, sliced
15ml/1 tbsp plain (all-purpose) flour
400ml/14fl oz/1⅔ cups dry (hard) cider
350g/12oz celeriac, cut into chunks
15ml/1 tbsp chopped fresh sage
15ml/1 tbsp Worcestershire sauce
2 small cooking apples, cored
salt and ground black pepper

1 Preheat the oven to 180°C/350°F/ Gas 4. Heat the oil in a frying pan, add the sausages and fry for 5 minutes. Transfer the sausages to an ovenproof dish and drain any excess oil from the pan to leave 15ml/1 tbsp. Add the onions and cook for a few minutes, stirring occasionally, until softened and turning golden.

2 Stir in the flour, then gradually add the cider and bring to the boil, stirring. Add the celeriac and stir in the sage, Worcestershire sauce and seasoning. Pour the cider and celeriac mixture over the sausages. Cover, put into the hot oven and cook for 30 minutes, or until the celeriac is soft.

3 Slice the apples, then stir into the casserole. Cover and cook for a further 10–15 minutes. Serve hot.

Per portion Energy 508kcal/2114kJ; Protein 12.7g; Carbohydrate 29.3g, of which sugars 13.6g; Fat 35.8g, of which saturates 12.3g; Cholesterol 45mg; Calcium 131mg; Fibre 3.3g; Sodium 1019mg.

Roast pork with apple and redcurrant jelly

Roasted apples with redcurrant jelly provides the perfect foil for roast pork and crackling.

Serves 8–10

1 bone-in pork loin, weighing
    about 2.25kg/5lb
10ml/2 tsp mustard powder
15 whole cloves
2 bay leaves
900ml/1½ pints/3¾ cups water
175ml/6fl oz/¾ cup single (light)
    cream (optional)
salt and ground white pepper
braised red cabbage, to serve

For the glazed potatoes

900g/2lb small potatoes
50g/2oz/¼ cup caster (superfine) sugar
65g/2½oz/5 tbsp butter

For the apples with redcurrant jelly

750ml/1¼ pints/3 cups water
115g/4oz/generous ½ cup soft
    light brown sugar
5ml/1 tsp lemon juice
4–5 tart apples, peeled, cored
    and halved
60–75ml/4–5 tbsp redcurrant jelly

1 Preheat the oven to 200°C/400°F/ Gas 6.

2 Use a sharp knife to score the pork skin with diagonal cuts to make a diamond pattern. Rub the rind with the salt, pepper and mustard powder. Push the cloves and bay leaves into the skin.

3 Place the pork loin, skin side up, on a rack in a roasting pan and cook for about 1 hour, until the skin is crisp and golden.

4 Pour the water into the bottom of the roasting pan and cook for a further 30 minutes.

5 For the glazed potatoes, boil the potatoes in salted water for 15–20 minutes, or until soft. Drain, peel and keep warm. Melt the sugar in a frying pan over a low heat until it turns light brown. Add the potatoes and butter, stirring to coat the potatoes, and cook for about 6–8 minutes, until the potatoes are a rich golden brown. Keep warm.

6 To cook the apples, bring the water to the boil in a large pan and stir in the brown sugar. Add the lemon juice and apple halves, lower the heat and poach gently until the apples are just tender. Remove the apples from the pan. Spoon 7.5ml/1½ tsp redcurrant jelly into the hollow of each apple half and keep warm.

7 When the pork is cooked, transfer it to a serving dish and leave it in a warm place to rest for 15 minutes before carving. Meanwhile, make the gravy. Transfer the roasting pan juices into a pan and reduce over a medium heat. Whisk in a little cream if you wish, and season with salt and pepper to taste.

8 Remove the crackling from the pork, and serve it separately, warm. Serve the pork with the gravy, caramelized potatoes, poached apple halves and braised red cabbage.

Per portion Energy 654kcal/2735kJ; Protein 36.9g; Carbohydrate 39.5g, of which sugars 26.2g; Fat 39.9g, of which saturates 16.1g; Cholesterol 124mg; Calcium 36mg; Fibre 1.5g; Sodium 152mg.

Spiced pork roast with apple and thyme cream sauce

Belly of pork (sometimes called 'lap' of pork) makes a tasty and tender roasting joint. In this unusual dish, the pork is boned and skinned for stuffing and rolling.

Serves 6
1 medium onion, finely chopped
3 garlic cloves, crushed
75g/3oz/6 tbsp butter
a bunch of mixed fresh herbs, leaves finely chopped
225g/8oz/4 cups fine fresh breadcrumbs
1 egg, beaten
1 piece of pork belly, about 1.3kg/3lb
15ml/1 tbsp vegetable oil
salt and ground black pepper
steamed green vegetables, to serve

For the spicy paste
25g/1oz/2 tbsp butter, melted
30ml/2 tbsp chutney
15ml/1 tbsp lemon juice
2 garlic cloves, crushed
30ml/2 tbsp mild wholegrain mustard

For the sauce
2 large cooking apples, peeled, cored and chopped
1 medium onion, chopped
2 garlic cloves, crushed
1 or 2 thyme sprigs
150ml/¼ pint/⅔ cup medium (hard) cider
about 150ml/¼ pint/⅔ cup chicken stock
300ml/½ pint/1¼ cups single (light) cream

1 Cook the onion and garlic in the butter until soft, then add the herbs and breadcrumbs. Cool a little before mixing in the egg, and season well with salt and ground pepper. Preheat the oven to 150°C/300°F/Gas 2.

2 Meanwhile, trim off any fat from the meat and prick the centre with a fork. Combine all the spicy paste ingredients together and brush the meat with this. Spread the stuffing all over the meat, then roll it up and secure it with cotton string.

3 Brown the meat in the oil in a hot roasting pan and cook in the oven for 3 hours. Halfway through cooking remove the joint from the oven and brush liberally with the remainder of the spicy paste; turn over, return the pan to the oven, and continue cooking.

4 To make the apple and thyme cream sauce, put the cooking apples, onion and garlic in a large pan and add the thyme sprigs, cider and stock. Bring to the boil and simmer gently for 15 minutes, then discard the thyme. Add the cream. Blend the mixture, strain and season to taste. If the sauce is too thick, add extra stock. Serve the sliced meat on heated plates with steamed green vegetables and the sauce.

Per portion Energy 814kcal/3409kJ; Protein 73.2g; Carbohydrate 41.9g, of which sugars 12.6g; Fat 39.8g, of which saturates 20.2g; Cholesterol 264mg; Calcium 145mg; Fibre 2.4g; Sodium 581mg.

Roast goose with apples

In Russia it is traditional to serve your guests roast goose with apples on New Year's Eve. The goose is served on a silver plate and carved at the table.

Serves 4–6
1 goose
8–10 Granny Smith apples, peeled, cored and cut into wedges
65g/2½oz/5 tbsp butter
200ml/7fl oz/scant 1 cup water
salt and ground black pepper
boiled or roasted potatoes with fresh dill, and boiled buckwheat, to serve

1 Preheat the oven to 180°C/350°F/ Gas 4. Season the goose inside and out. Peel, core and quarter four of the apples and stuff them inside the neck end of the goose. Fold the neck skin over then truss the goose, making sure that the legs are close to the body.

2 Weigh the goose to work out the cooking time, and calculate 15 minutes per 450g/1lb, plus 15 minutes further.

3 Grease a roasting pan with 25g/1oz/ 2 tbsp of the butter. Put the goose in the pan. Melt the rest of the butter and brush over the goose. Pour the water around the goose. Cook for 1½ hours.

4 Remove the cores from the remaining apples.

5 Put the whole apples around the goose and bake for the remainder of the cooking time. The goose is cooked when a skewer is pierced into the thickest part of a leg and the juices come out clear.

6 Transfer the goose to a platter. Remove the stuffing, carve, and serve with the potatoes and boiled buckwheat.

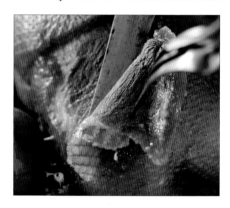

Per portion Energy 822kcal/3437kJ; Protein 54.8g; Carbohydrate 44.1g, of which sugars 21.8g; Fat 48.7g, of which saturates 0.9g; Cholesterol 0mg; Calcium 87mg; Fibre 3.1g; Sodium 486mg.

Grouse with orchard fruit stuffing

Tart apples, plums and pears, with a hint of spice, make a fabulous orchard fruit stuffing that complements the rich gamey flavour of grouse perfectly.

Serves 2
juice of ½ lemon
2 young grouse
50g/2oz/¼ cup butter
4 Swiss chard leaves
50ml/2fl oz/¼ cup Marsala
salt and ground black pepper

For the stuffing
2 shallots, finely chopped
1 cooking apple, peeled, cored and chopped
1 pear, peeled, cored and chopped
2 plums, halved, stoned (pitted) and chopped
a large pinch of mixed (apple pie) spice

1 Sprinkle the lemon juice over the grouse and season them with salt and freshly ground black pepper.

2 Melt half the butter in a large flameproof casserole, add the grouse and cook for 10 minutes, or until browned, turning occasionally. Use tongs to remove the grouse from the casserole and set aside.

Cook's tip
There isn't a lot of liquid in the casserole for cooking the birds – they are steamed rather than boiled, so it is very important that the casserole is heavy with a tight-fitting lid, otherwise the liquid may evaporate and the chard burn on the base of the pan.

3 Add the shallots to the fat remaining in the casserole and cook until they are softened but not coloured.

4 Add the apple, pear, plums and a generous pinch of mixed spice and cook for approximately 5 minutes, or until the fruits are just beginning to soften.

5 Remove the casserole from the heat and spoon the hot fruit mixture into the body cavities of the birds.

6 Truss the grouse neatly with string. Smear the remaining butter over the birds and wrap them in the chard leaves. Replace them in the casserole.

7 Pour in the Marsala and heat until simmering. Cover tightly and simmer for 20 minutes, or until the birds are tender, taking care not to overcook them. Leave to rest in a warm place for about 10 minutes before serving.

Per portion: Energy 521kcal/2191kJ; Protein 76.5g; Carbohydrate 17.5g, of which sugars 17.3g; Fat 13.5g, of which saturates 2.9g; Cholesterol 0mg; Calcium 302mg; Fibre 5.8g; Sodium 404mg.

Slow-roast belly of wild boar with apple

There are those who love fat and those who do not. This recipe can be enjoyed by both, as wild boar is much less fatty than its domestic cousins and this slow-cooked method renders much of what fat there is, basting the flesh as it cooks to leave a soft-textured meat with a lip-smacking stickiness. The tart apple complements the rich pork.

Serves 4

1.3kg/3lb wild boar belly, skin scored
15ml/1 tbsp olive oil
4 firm, tart green apples
50g/2oz/¼ cup butter
50g/2oz/¼ cup demerara (raw) sugar
a sprig of thyme, plus extra for garnish
3 heads chicory (Belgian endive),
  2 white, 1 red, outer leaves and
  stems removed, leaves separated

For the salad dressing

10ml/2 tsp Dijon mustard
10ml/2 tsp maple syrup
5ml/1 tsp cider vinegar
30ml/2 tbsp light olive oil
salt and ground black pepper

1 Preheat the oven to 150°C/300°F/ Gas 2. Rub the pork all over with the olive oil and salt and pepper, rubbing it into the scores in the skin.

2 Place the pork, skin side up, in a sturdy roasting pan. Sprinkle the skin with extra salt. Place in the oven for 3½–4 hours, until the meat is cooked.

3 To make the salad dressing, put the mustard, maple syrup and vinegar in a bowl and whisk together. Gently drizzle in the light olive oil, whisking as you go to emulsify the ingredients. Season with salt and pepper.

4 When the meat has been cooking for 3 hours, prepare the apples. Halve them horizontally, remove the cores and pips (seeds) with a spoon, and set aside.

5 In a heavy frying pan, gently heat the butter, sugar and thyme leaves, stirring, until the sugar and butter have melted.

6 Place the apples cut side down in the mixture and cook gently for 5 minutes, moving them in the pan occasionally. Turn the apples, cover, and cook for a further 10–15 minutes, until softening. Remove from the pan and keep warm.

7 When the belly is cooked, remove from the oven and leave to rest for 10 minutes. Carve into eight slices, two for each serving.

8 Arrange the meat on warm plates with two halves of apple each and some chicory leaves. Drizzle the chicory with the maple and mustard dressing and garnish with thyme.

Per portion Energy 1499kcal/6203kJ; Protein 50.6g; Carbohydrate 24.1g, of which sugars 22.4g; Fat 134.6g, of which saturates 50.7g; Cholesterol 263mg; Calcium 56mg; Fibre 1.9g; Sodium 415mg.

Quail with apples

These tiny birds have very short cooking times, and increasingly appear in restaurants and domestic kitchens.

**Serves 2 as a main course
   or 4 as a first course**
2 firm eating apples
4 oven-ready quail
120ml/4fl oz/½ cup olive oil
115g/4oz/½ cup butter
4 slices white bread
salt and ground black pepper

1 Preheat the oven to 220°C/425°F/ Gas 7. Core the apples and slice them thickly (leave the peel on if it is pretty and not too tough).

2 Brush the quail with half the olive oil and roast them in a pan in the oven for 10 minutes, or until brown and tender.

3 Meanwhile, heat half the butter in a frying pan and sauté the apple slices for about 3 minutes until they are golden but not mushy. Season with pepper, cover and keep warm until required.

4 Remove the crusts from the bread. Heat the remaining olive oil and the butter in a frying pan and fry the bread on both sides until brown and crisp.

5 Lay the fried bread on heated plates and place the quail on top. Arrange the fried apple slices around them, and serve immediately.

Per portion Energy 814kcal/3389kJ; Protein 53.3g; Carbohydrate 33.3g, of which sugars 10.5g; Fat 43.6g, of which saturates 23.4g; Cholesterol 69mg; Calcium 169mg; Fibre 2.4g; Sodium 644mg.

Pheasant breast with apples

This classic French recipe contains apples, Calvados and rich cream.

Serves 2
2 boneless pheasant breasts
30g/1oz/2 tbsp butter
1 onion, thinly sliced
1 eating apple, peeled and quartered
10ml/2 tsp sugar
60ml/4 tbsp Calvados
60ml/4 tbsp chicken stock
1.5ml/¼ tsp dried thyme
1.5ml/¼ tsp white pepper
125ml/4fl oz/½ cup whipping cream
salt
sautéed potatoes, to serve

1 With a sharp knife, score the thick end of each pheasant breast. In a heavy frying pan melt half the butter over a medium heat. Add the onion and cook for 8–10 minutes until golden, stirring occasionally. Using a slotted spoon, transfer the onion to a plate.

2 Cut each apple quarter crossways into thin slices. Melt half of the remaining butter in the pan and add the apple slices. Sprinkle with the sugar and cook the apple slices slowly for 5–7 minutes until golden and caramelized, turning occasionally. Transfer the apples to the plate with the onion, then wipe out the pan.

3 Add the remaining butter to the pan and increase the heat to medium-high. Add the pheasant breasts, skin side down, and cook for 3–4 minutes until golden. Turn and cook for a further 1–2 minutes until the juices run slightly pink when the thickest part of the meat is pierced with a knife. Transfer to a board and cover to keep warm.

4 Add the Calvados to the pan and boil over a high heat until reduced by half. Add the stock, thyme, a little salt and the white pepper and reduce by half again. Stir in the cream, bring to the boil and cook for 1 minute. Add the reserved onion and apple slices to the pan and cook for 1 minute.

5 Slice each pheasant breast diagonally and arrange on warmed plates. Spoon over a little sauce with the onion and apples.

> **Cook's tip**
> If you can't find Calvados, substitute Cognac, cider or apple juice instead.

Per portion Energy 629kcal/2611kJ; Protein 19g; Carbohydrate 29g, of which sugars 27g; Fat 45g, of which saturates 26g; Cholesterol 230mg; Calcium 81mg; Fibre 2g; Sodium 387mg.

DESSERTS

Sweet and juicy or tart and crunchy, apples are a wonderfully versatile and healthy option for many hot or cold desserts. Choose from traditional favourites such as Apple and Blackberry Crumble or Eve's Pudding, or more unusual desserts such as Apple Snow or Apple and Lemon Risotto with Poached Plums.

Frozen apple and blackberry terrine

This pretty autumn fruit terrine is frozen so that you can enjoy a healthy dessert at any time of the year.

Serves 6

450g/1lb cooking or eating apples
300ml/½ pint/1¼ cups sweet (hard) cider
15ml/1 tbsp clear honey
5ml/1 tsp vanilla extract
200g/7oz/scant 2 cups fresh or frozen and thawed blackberries
15ml/1 tbsp powdered gelatine
2 egg whites
fresh apple slices and blackberries, to decorate

1 Peel, core and chop the apples and place them in a pan with half the cider. Bring the cider to the boil, then lower the heat, cover the pan and let the apples simmer gently until tender.

2 Transfer the apples to a food processor and process them to a smooth purée. Stir in the honey and vanilla extract. Add half the blackberries to half the apple purée, and process again. Press through a sieve (strainer) to remove the seeds.

3 Heat the remaining cider until almost boiling, then sprinkle the gelatine over and stir until the gelatine has dissolved completely.

4 Add half the gelatine mixture to the apple purée and half to the blackberry and apple purée. Leave both purées to cool until almost set. Whisk the egg whites until stiff. Quickly fold them into the apple purée.

5 Stir the remaining whole blackberries into half the apple purée, and then transfer this to a 1.75 litre/3 pint/7½ cup loaf tin (pan), packing it in firmly.

6 Top with the blackberry purée and spread it evenly. Finally, add a layer of the plain apple purée and smooth it evenly. If necessary, freeze each layer until firm before adding the next.

7 Freeze until firm. To serve, remove from the freezer and allow to stand at room temperature for 20 minutes to soften. Serve in slices, decorated with apples slices and blackberries.

Per portion Energy 67kcal/283kJ; Protein 1.5g; Carbohydrate 12.4g, of which sugars 12.4g; Fat 0.2g, of which saturates 0g; Cholesterol 0mg; Calcium 21mg; Fibre 2.2g; Sodium 26mg.

Apple ice cream with cinnamon bread

Cooking apples with butter, lemon and spice accentuates their flavour and makes a marvellous ice cream.

Serves 2
675g/1½lb cooking apples
50g/2oz/¼ cup unsalted butter
1.5ml/¼ tsp mixed (apple pie) spice
finely grated rind and juice of 1 lemon
90g/3½oz/scant ½ cup cream cheese
2 egg whites, beaten
150ml/¼ pint/⅔ cup double (heavy) cream
mint sprigs, to decorate

For the cinnamon bread
6 thick slices of white bread
1 egg, beaten
1 egg yolk
2.5ml/½ tsp vanilla extract
150ml/¼ pint/⅔ cup single (light) cream
65g/2½oz/5 tbsp caster (superfine) sugar
2.5ml/½ tsp ground cinnamon
25g/1oz/2 tbsp unsalted butter
45ml/3 tbsp vegetable oil

1 Peel, core and slice the apples. Melt the butter in a pan. Add the apple slices, mixed spice and lemon rind. Cover and cook gently for 10 minutes until the apples are soft. Leave to cool.

2 Put the apples into a food processor. Add the lemon juice and cream cheese. Blend until smooth. In separate bowls, whisk the egg whites until stiff and the cream until it forms soft peaks.

3 Scrape the purée into a bowl. Fold in the cream, then the egg whites. Spoon into a plastic tub and freeze overnight.

4 Make the cinnamon bread about 20 minutes before serving. Cut the crusts off the bread slices, then cut each slice diagonally in half. Beat together the egg, egg yolk, vanilla extract, cream and 15ml/1 tbsp of the sugar.

5 Arrange the bread triangles in a single layer on a large, shallow plate or tray. Pour the cream mixture over the bread triangles and leave for about 10 minutes until the mixture has been thoroughly absorbed.

6 Mix the remaining sugar with the cinnamon on a plate. Melt the butter with the oil in a large frying pan. When it is hot, add half the bread and fry until golden underneath. Turn the slices with a metal spatula and fry the other side.

7 Drain the slices lightly on kitchen paper, then coat them on both sides in the cinnamon sugar and keep them hot. Cook the remaining slices in the same way. Serve at once, topped with scoops of the apple ice cream and decorated with the mint sprigs.

Per portion Energy 535kcal/2227kJ; Protein 5.7g; Carbohydrate 34.7g, of which sugars 23g; Fat 42.6g, of which saturates 23.3g; Cholesterol 123mg; Calcium 94mg; Fibre 2.2g; Sodium 288mg.

Apple and cider water ice

This very English combination has a subtle apple flavour with just a hint of cider. As the apple purée is very pale, almost white, add a few drops of green food colouring to echo the pale green skin of the Granny Smith apples.

Serves 6
500g/1¼lb Granny Smith apples
150g/5oz/¾ cup caster (superfine) sugar
300ml/½ pint/1¼ cups water
250ml/8fl oz/1 cup strong dry (hard) cider
few drops of green food colouring (optional)
strips of thinly pared lime rind, to decorate

1 Quarter, core and roughly chop the apples. Put them into a pan. Add the caster sugar and half the water. Cover and simmer for 10 minutes or until the apples are soft.

2 Press the mixture through a sieve (strainer) placed over a bowl. Discard the apple skins. Stir the cider and the remaining water into the apple purée and add a little colouring, if you like.

3 Pour into a shallow plastic container and freeze for 6 hours, beating with a fork once or twice to break up the ice crystals.

4 Scoop into dishes and decorate with twists of thinly pared lime rind.

Per portion Energy 143kcal/610kJ; Protein 0.4g; Carbohydrate 34.6g, of which sugars 34.6g; Fat 0.1g, of which saturates 0g; Cholesterol 0mg; Calcium 20mg; Fibre 1.3g; Sodium 6mg.

Apple and blueberry fool

Using dessert apples instead of cooking apples introduces a naturally sweet flavour, so no added sugar is needed.

Serves 6–8
450g/1lb sweet eating apples
450g/1lb/4 cups blueberries or bilberries
juice of 1 lemon
1 sachet powdered gelatine
2 egg whites
60ml/4 tbsp double (heavy) cream, whipped to serve

1 Peel, core and slice the apples. Put them in a large pan with the bilberries and 150ml/¼ pint/⅔ cup water. Cook the fruit for 15 minutes. Remove from the heat.

2 Strain the lemon juice into a cup, sprinkle the gelatine over and leave it to soak. When the gelatine has dissolved mix it into the fruit.

3 Turn the fruit mixture into a nylon sieve (strainer) over a large mixing bowl and press the fruit through it to make a purée; discard anything that is left in the sieve. Leave the purée to stand until it is cool and beginning to set.

4 Whisk the egg whites until they are standing in soft peaks.

5 Using a metal spoon, fold the whites gently into the fruit purée to make a smooth mousse. Turn into serving glasses and chill until set. Serve topped with the whipped cream.

Per portion Energy 92kcal/385kJ; Protein 1.6g; Carbohydrate 13g, of which sugars 10.8g; Fat 4.1g, of which saturates 2.5g; Cholesterol 10mg; Calcium 6mg; Fibre 2g; Sodium 18mg.

Apple snow

This fluffy nursery dish is as simple as it is delicious – and best made with late-cropping Bramley's Seedling cooking apples, which grow abundantly in Britain and 'fall' when cooked, to make a fluffy purée. Serve with crisp cookies, or sponge fingers.

Serves 6
675g/1½lb cooking apples, preferably Bramley's Seedling
a little thinly peeled lemon rind
about 115g/4oz/generous ½ cup caster (superfine) sugar
3 egg whites

1 Peel, core and slice the apples. Place in a pan with 45ml/3 tbsp water and the lemon rind. Cover and simmer gently for 15 minutes, or until the apples become fluffy. Remove from the heat, take out the lemon rind and sweeten to taste with caster sugar.

2 Beat the apples well with a wooden spoon to make a purée, or rub through a sieve (strainer) if a smoother texture is preferred. Leave to cool.

3 When the purée is cold, whisk the egg whites until stiff.

4 Fold the egg whites into the apple using a metal spoon. Whisk together until the mixture is thick and light.

5 Turn into a serving bowl, or divide between six individual dishes, and chill until required.

Per portion Energy 121kcal/516kJ; Protein 1.8g; Carbohydrate 30.1g, of which sugars 30.1g; Fat 0.1g, of which saturates 0g; Cholesterol 0mg; Calcium 7mg; Fibre 1.8g; Sodium 34mg.

Brandied apple Charlotte

Loosely based on a traditional Apple Charlotte recipe, this iced version combines brandy-steeped dried apple with a spicy ricotta cream to make an unusual and inspiring dessert.

Serves 8–10
130g/4½oz/¾ cup dried apples
75ml/5 tbsp brandy
50g/2oz/¼ cup unsalted butter
115g/4oz/½ cup light muscovado
    (brown) sugar
2.5ml/½ tsp mixed (apple pie) spice
60ml/4 tbsp water
75g/3oz/½ cup sultanas (golden raisins)
300g/11oz Madeira cake, cut into
    1cm/½in slices
250g/9oz/generous 1 cup ricotta cheese
30ml/2 tbsp lemon juice
150ml/¼ pint/⅔ cup double (heavy) or
    whipping cream
icing (confectioners') sugar and fresh
    mint sprigs, to decorate

1 Roughly chop the dried apples, then transfer them to a clean bowl. Pour over the brandy and set aside for about 1 hour or until most of the brandy has been absorbed.

2 Melt the butter in a frying pan. Add the sugar and stir over a low heat for 1 minute.

3 Add the mixed spice, water and soaked apples, with any remaining brandy. Heat until just simmering, reduce the heat slightly, if necessary, and then cook gently for about 5 minutes or until the apples are tender. Stir in the sultanas, take off the heat and leave the mixture to cool completely.

4 Use the Madeira cake slices to line the sides of a 20cm/8in square or 20cm/8in round springform or loose-based cake tin (pan). Place in the freezer while you make the filling.

5 Beat the ricotta in a bowl until it has softened, then stir in the apple mixture and lemon juice. Whip the cream in a separate bowl and fold it in. Spoon the mixture into the lined tin and level the surface. Cover and freeze overnight.

6 Transfer the apple Charlotte to the refrigerator 1 hour before serving. Invert it on to a serving plate, dust with sugar, and decorate with mint sprigs.

Cook's tip
Line the tin with clear film (plastic wrap) before placing the cake in it to help the dessert turn out more easily,

---

Per portion Energy 446kcal/1869kJ; Protein 6g; Carbohydrate 54.4g, of which sugars 46.2g; Fat 21.9g, of which saturates 13.3g; Cholesterol 49mg; Calcium 119mg; Fibre 2.1g; Sodium 222mg.

Apple and almond cheesecake

This isn't a typical cheesecake, more of a cheese and apple pie. It has plenty of flavour and is perfect served with a summer berry coulis.

Serves 8

250g/9oz/generous 1 cup cream cheese
250g/9oz/generous 1 cup ricotta cheese
4 eggs, separated
75g/3oz/⅔ cup semolina flour
30ml/2 tbsp ground almonds
200ml/7fl oz/scant 1 cup sour cream
115g/4oz/generous ½ cup caster (superfine) sugar
5 eating apples, peeled, cored and thinly sliced
grated rind and juice of 1 lemon
115g/4oz/1 cup flaked (sliced) almonds
250g/9oz/generous 2 cups berries (any that are in season)
10ml/2 tsp sugar

1 Preheat the oven to 180°C/350°F/ Gas 4. Butter and line a 20 × 30cm/ 8 × 12in cake tin (pan).

2 Put the cream cheese and ricotta cheese in a large bowl and mix well. Add the egg yolks one at a time, stirring each into the cheese mixture.

3 Sprinkle the semolina flour over the top and stir in, then add the ground almonds, followed by the sour cream and sugar.

4 Put the egg whites into a clean, grease-free bowl and whisk until they form stiff peaks. Stir two large spoonfuls into the cheese mixture, then fold in the remainder.

5 Put the apples into a large bowl. Add the lemon juice and rind, and mix well to coat. (The juice will protect the apples from discoloration and add flavour.) Add the apples to the cheese mixture and fold in. Transfer to the prepared tin and sprinkle with the flaked almonds. Bake for 40 minutes, or until the top is golden brown.

6 While the cheesecake is baking in the oven, put the berries in a small pan with the sugar and 15–30ml/1–2 tbsp water. Simmer the fruit for 5–6 minutes, or until just softened. Purée the berries in a blender, then pass through a fine sieve (strainer) and leave to cool. Serve the cheesecake warm topped with a generous dollop of the berry coulis.

Per portion Energy 500kcal/2080kJ; Protein 12.8g; Carbohydrate 30.1g, of which sugars 22.3g; Fat 37.5g, of which saturates 16.9g; Cholesterol 153mg; Calcium 124mg; Fibre 2.4g; Sodium 145mg.

Apple-stuffed crêpes

Light, fluffy crêpes, filled with sweet, sugary apple slices, combine to make a delicious summertime dessert.

Serves 4
115g/4oz/1 cup plain (all-purpose) flour
a pinch of salt
2 large (US extra large) eggs
175ml/6fl oz/¾ cup milk
120ml/4fl oz/½ cup sweet (hard) cider
butter, for frying
4 eating apples
60ml/4 tbsp caster (superfine) sugar
120ml/8 tbsp clear honey, and 150ml/
 ¼ pint/⅔ cup double (heavy) cream,
 to serve

1 Make the batter. Sift the flour and salt into a large bowl. Add the eggs and milk and beat until smooth. Stir in the cider. Leave to stand for 30 minutes.

2 Heat a small heavy non-stick frying pan. Add a little butter and ladle in enough batter to coat the pan thinly.

3 Cook the crêpe for about 1 minute until it is golden underneath, then flip it over and cook the other side until golden. Slide the crêpe on to a plate, then repeat with the remaining batter to make seven more. Set the crêpes aside and keep warm.

4 Make the apple filling. Core the apples and cut them into thick slices. Heat 15g/½oz butter in a large frying pan. Add the apples to the pan and cook until golden on both sides. Transfer the slices to a bowl with a slotted spoon and sprinkle with sugar.

5 Fold each pancake in half, then fold in half again to form a cone. Fill each with some of the fried apples. Place two filled pancakes on each dessert plate. Drizzle with a little honey and serve at once, accompanied by cream.

Cook's tip
For the best results, use full-fat (whole) milk in the batter.

Per portion Energy 489kcal/2057kJ; Protein 8.2g; Carbohydrate 71.5g, of which sugars 49.6g; Fat 20.1g, of which saturates 11.3g; Cholesterol 139mg; Calcium 137mg; Fibre 2.1g; Sodium 69mg.

Baked apple dumplings

A treat good enough for any special occasion. The sharpness of the fruit contrasts perfectly with the maple syrup drizzled over this delightful pastry parcel.

Serves 8
8 firm cooking apples, peeled
1 egg white
130g/4½oz/⅔ cup caster (superfine) sugar
45ml/3 tbsp double (heavy) cream, plus extra whipped cream, to serve
2.5m/½ tsp vanilla extract
250ml/8fl oz/1 cup maple syrup

For the pastry
475g/1lb 2oz/4½ cups plain (all-purpose) flour
2.5ml/½ tsp salt
350g/12oz/1½ cups butter or white vegetable fat, diced
175–250ml/6–8fl oz/¾–1 cup chilled water

1 To make the pastry, sift the flour and salt into a large bowl. Rub or cut in the butter or fat until the mixture resembles fine breadcrumbs.

2 Sprinkle over 175ml/6fl oz/¾ cup water and mix until the dough holds together, adding a little more water if necessary. Gather into a ball. Wrap the dough in clear film (plastic wrap) and chill for at least 20 minutes. Preheat the oven to 220°C/425°F/Gas 7.

3 Cutting from the stem end, core the apples without cutting through the base. Roll out the pastry thinly. Cut squares almost large enough to enclose the apples; brush with egg white and set an apple in the centre of each. Cut pastry rounds to cover the tops of the apples. Reserve the trimmings. Combine the sugar, cream and vanilla extract in a small bowl. Spoon into the hollow of each apple.

4 Place a pastry circle on top of each apple, then bring up the sides of the pastry square to enclose it, pleating the larger piece of pastry to make a snug fit around the apple. Moisten the joins where they overlap.

5 Make apple stalks and leaves from the pastry trimmings and decorate the tops of the dumplings.

6 Set them in a large greased baking dish, at least 2cm/¾in apart. Bake for 30 minutes, then lower the oven temperature to 180°C/350°F/Gas 4 and continue baking for 20 minutes more until the pastry is golden brown and the apples are tender.

7 Transfer the dumplings to a serving dish. Mix the maple syrup with the juices in the baking dish and drizzle over the dumplings. Serve hot.

Cook's tip
Egg yolk glaze brushed on to the pastry gives it a nice golden sheen.

Per portion Energy 713kcal/2988kJ; Protein 6.6g; Carbohydrate 94.7g, of which sugars 49.5g; Fat 36.8g, of which saturates 22.9g; Cholesterol 93mg; Calcium 108mg; Fibre 3g; Sodium 361mg.

Baked apples with marzipan

This is a traditional recipe for the winter, when apples were once the only fresh fruits available and cooks needed to be really creative to find different ways to serve them. It's a comforting hot dessert: when you eat it you won't mind at all that the range of local fruit is so small at this time of year.

Serves 4
25g/1oz/¼ cup raisins
10ml/2 tsp brandy
4 large, crisp eating apples,
    such as Braeburn
75g/3oz marzipan, chopped
juice of ½ lemon
20g/¾oz/¼ cup chopped pistachio nuts
single (light) cream, to serve

1 Preheat the oven to 160°C/325°F/ Gas 3. Soak the raisins in the brandy for 20 minutes. Meanwhile, core the apples. Cut a small slice off the bottom of each one, if necessary, so that they will stand up. Score the skin around the apple in three places to prevent it rolling up during baking.

2 Mix the marzipan with the lemon juice, chopped pistachio nuts and raisins, and push the filling into the centre of the apples. Put the apples on a baking tray lined with baking parchment, and bake them for 20–25 minutes, until tender. Serve the apples warm with a splash of cream.

Per portion Energy 150kcal/631kJ; Protein 2.2g; Carbohydrate 22.9g, of which sugars 22.7g; Fat 5.3g, of which saturates 0.6g; Cholesterol 0mg; Calcium 23mg; Fibre 2.3g; Sodium 33mg.

Caramel apples

These delicious treats are popular at fairs and fêtes around the world. The buttery, chewy caramel contrasts wonderfully with the crisp apple.

Serves 8
8 small or medium eating apples
115g/4oz/½ cup unsalted butter
200g/7oz/1 cup granulated (white) sugar
150ml/¼ pint/⅔ cup double (heavy) cream
15ml/1 tbsp soft light brown sugar
125g/4¼oz/⅓ cup golden (light corn) syrup
2.5ml/½ tsp vanilla extract
1.5ml/¼ tsp salt

1 Wash and dry the apples. Push lollipop sticks or wooden dowels into the stem-end of the apples.

2 Prepare an ice-water bath and line a shallow baking tray with a sheet of baking parchment.

3 Place all of the remaining ingredients in a large, heavy pan and heat them gently over a medium heat. Stir to dissolve everything together into an emulsified mass.

4 Once the sugar has completely dissolved, bring the mixture to the boil and cook until it reaches the soft-ball stage (114°C/238°F).

5 Remove the caramel from the heat and arrest the cooking by placing the pan over the ice-water bath.

6 Leave the mixture to cool to 82°C/180°F before dipping the apples into the caramel, holding them by their sticks.

7 Place the caramel-covered apples on the parchment-lined baking sheet, stick or dowel end up, and allow them to cool.

8 If the caramel slips off the apple at all, leave it to cool slightly and dip again. Eat immediately or store in an airtight container at room temperature for up to 3 days.

Per portion Energy 366kcal/1534kJ; Protein 0.8g; Carbohydrate 46.9g, of which sugars 46.9g; Fat 21.9g, of which saturates 13.4g; Cholesterol 57mg; Calcium 33mg; Fibre 1.1g; Sodium 160mg.

Apple and blackberry crumble

Autumn heralds the harvest of apples and succulent soft fruits. The pinhead oatmeal in the topping makes this traditional hot dessert especially crunchy and flavoursome.

Serves 6–8
900g/2lb cooking apples
450g/1lb/4 cups blackberries
a squeeze of lemon juice (optional)
175g/6oz/scant 1 cup sugar

For the topping
115g/4oz/½ cup butter
115g/4oz/1 cup wholemeal
 (whole-wheat) flour
50g/2oz/½ cup fine or medium
 pinhead oatmeal
50g/2oz/¼ cup soft light brown sugar
a little grated lemon rind (optional)

1 Preheat the oven to 200°C/400°F/ Gas 6.

2 Rub the butter into the flour, and then add the oatmeal and brown sugar. Continue to rub in until the mixture begins to stick together, forming large crumbs. Mix in the grated lemon rind.

3 Peel, core and slice the cooking apples into wedges.

4 Put the fruit, lemon juice (if using), 30ml/2 tbsp water and the sugar into a shallow ovenproof dish.

5 Cover the fruit with the topping. Sprinkle with a little cold water. Bake in the oven for 15 minutes, then reduce the heat to 190°C/375°F/Gas 5 and cook for another 15–20 minutes until crunchy and brown on top. Serve hot with chilled crème fraîche or ice cream.

Per portion Energy 470kcal/1974kJ; Protein 5.1g; Carbohydrate 78.2g, of which sugars 60.3g; Fat 17.2g, of which saturates 10g; Cholesterol 41mg; Calcium 71mg; Fibre 7g; Sodium 128mg.

Baked apples with cinnamon and nuts

This cinnamon-sweet light dessert is one for the health conscious.

Serves 4
4 large, firm cooking apples
15g/½oz/1 tbsp butter
vanilla ice cream, to serve

For the filling
25g/1oz/2 tbsp butter
90ml/6 tbsp blanched almonds
30ml/2 tbsp sugar
5ml/1 tsp ground cinnamon

1 Preheat the oven to 220°C/425°F/ Gas 7.

2 To make the filling, melt the butter. Grind or finely chop the almonds and put in a bowl. Using a wooden spoon, add the sugar, cinnamon and melted butter and mix together.

3 Peel the apples and remove the cores, leaving the apples intact at the bottom so that the filling will not run out. Put the apples in an ovenproof dish.

4 Stuff the apples evenly. Melt the butter in a small pan and pour over the apples to coat.

5 Bake the apples in the oven for about 20 minutes, until the apples are soft, but before they collapse. Serve hot, with vanilla ice cream.

Per portion Energy 294kcal/1229kJ; Protein 5.3g; Carbohydrate 22.8g, of which sugars 22.2g; Fat 20.9g, of which saturates 6.2g; Cholesterol 21mg; Calcium 66mg; Fibre 4.1g; Sodium 67mg.

Hot blackberry and apple soufflés

As the blackberry season is so short and the apple season so long, it's always worth freezing a bag of blackberries to have on hand for making treats like this one.

Serves 6
butter, for greasing
150g/5oz/⅔ cup caster (superfine) sugar, plus extra for dusting
350g/12oz/3 cups blackberries
1 large cooking apple, peeled, cored and finely diced
grated rind and juice of 1 orange
3 egg whites
icing (confectioner's) sugar, for dusting

1 Preheat the oven to 200°C/400°F/ Gas 6. Put a baking sheet in the oven to heat. Generously grease six 150ml/ ¼ pint/⅔ cup individual soufflé dishes with butter and dust with caster sugar, shaking out the excess sugar.

2 Put the blackberries and diced apple in a pan with the orange rind. Squeeze the juice from the orange into the pan and cook for 10 minutes or until the apple has pulped down well.

3 Press through a sieve (strainer) into a bowl. Stir in 50g/2oz/¼ cup of the caster sugar. Set aside to cool.

4 Put a spoonful of the fruit purée into each prepared dish and smooth the surface. Set the dishes aside.

5 Whisk the egg whites in a large grease-free bowl until they form stiff peaks. Very gradually whisk in the remaining caster sugar to make a stiff, glossy meringue mixture.

6 Fold in the remaining fruit purée and spoon the flavoured meringue into the prepared dishes. Level the tops with a palette knife, and run a table knife around the edge of each dish.

7 Place the dishes on the hot baking sheet and bake for 10–15 minutes until the soufflés have risen well and are lightly browned. Dust the tops with icing sugar and serve immediately.

Per portion Energy 123kcal/522kJ; Protein 2.1g; Carbohydrate 30.1g, of which sugars 30.1g; Fat 0.1g, of which saturates 0g; Cholesterol 0mg; Calcium 38mg; Fibre 2g; Sodium 33mg.

Apple fritters with fruit compote

Hot fruit fritters are a popular dessert and are very quick and easy to make.

Serves 4
200g/7oz/1¾ cups self-raising (self-rising) flour
100ml/3½ fl oz/scant ½ cup milk
5ml/1 tsp baking powder
40g/1½oz/3 tbsp caster (superfine) sugar
a pinch of salt
5ml/1 tsp butter
2 eating apples
vegetable oil, for deep-frying
icing (confectioners') sugar, to dust
mixed berry compote, to serve

1 Mix the flour and milk in a bowl and add the baking powder, sugar and salt. Melt the butter in a small pan until it starts to brown, then mix it into the batter.

2 Heat the oil in a deep-fryer to 180°C/350°F.

3 Peel and core the apples and cut them into thick rings. Dip them in the batter, making sure that they are completely covered, then drop them straight into the hot oil and deep-fry for approximately 2–3 minutes, until the batter is crisp and golden brown.

4 Drain the fritters on kitchen paper, dust with icing sugar and serve immediately with the berry compote.

Per portion Energy 391kcal/1644kJ; Protein 5.5g; Carbohydrate 54g, of which sugars 16.8g; Fat 18.6g, of which saturates 2.8g; Cholesterol 4mg; Calcium 213mg; Fibre 2.4g; Sodium 205mg.

Apple pudding

3 Put the milk, butter and flour in a pan. Stirring continuously with a whisk, cook over medium heat until the sauce thickens and comes to the boil. Let it bubble gently for 1–2 minutes, stirring well to make sure it does not stick and burn on the bottom of the pan.

4 Pour into a bowl, add the sugar and vanilla extract, and then whisk in the egg yolks.

5 In a separate bowl, whisk the egg whites until stiff peaks form. With a large metal spoon, fold the egg whites into the custard. Pour the custard mixture over the apples in the dish.

6 Put into the hot oven and cook for about 40 minutes until puffed up, deep golden brown and firm to the touch. Serve straight out of the oven, before the soufflé-like topping begins to fall.

Per portion Energy 240kcal/1006kJ; Protein 7g; Carbohydrate 26.8g, of which sugars 19.2g; Fat 12.5g, of which saturates 6.8g; Cholesterol 121mg; Calcium 127mg; Fibre 1.9g; Sodium 131mg.

This deliciously light soufflé-like dessert is made here with an apple base, but there are plenty of other fruits you could choose from.

Serves 4
4 crisp eating apples
a little lemon juice
300ml/½ pint/1¼ cups milk
40g/1½oz/3 tbsp butter
40g/1½oz/⅓ cup plain (all-purpose) flour
25g/1oz/2 tbsp caster (superfine) sugar
2.5ml/½ tsp vanilla extract
2 eggs, separated

Variations
Stewed fruit, such as plums, rhubarb or gooseberries sweetened with honey or sugar would also make a good base.

1 Preheat the oven to 200°C/400°F/ Gas 6. Butter an ovenproof dish that is 20–23cm/8–9in in diameter and 5cm/2in deep.

2 Peel, core and slice the apples. Toss them with the lemon juice and cover the bottom of the buttered ovenproof dish.

Apple and kumquat sponge puddings

The intense flavour of kumquats makes these dainty puddings special. Served with more kumquats in a creamy sauce, this is a dessert that is sure to please.

Serves 8
150g/5oz/10 tbsp butter, at room
  temperature, plus extra for greasing
175g/6oz cooking apples, peeled and
  thinly sliced
75g/3oz kumquats, thinly sliced
150g/5oz/¾ cup golden caster
  (superfine) sugar
2 eggs
115g/4oz/1 cup self-raising
  (self-rising) flour

For the sauce
75g/3oz kumquats, thinly sliced
75g/3oz/6 tbsp caster (superfine) sugar
250ml/8fl oz/1 cup water
150ml/¼ pint/⅔ cup crème fraîche
5ml/1 tsp cornflour (cornstarch) mixed
  with 10ml/2 tsp water
lemon juice, to taste

1 Prepare a steamer. Butter eight 150ml/¼ pint/⅔ cup dariole moulds or ramekins and put a disc of buttered baking parchment on the base of each.

2 Melt 25g/1oz/2 tbsp butter in a frying pan. Add the apples, kumquats and 25g/1oz/2 tbsp sugar and cook over medium heat for 5–8 minutes, or until the apples start to soften and the sugar begins to caramelize. Remove from the heat and leave to cool.

3 Cream the remaining butter with the remaining sugar until pale and fluffy. Add the eggs, one at a time, beating after each addition. Fold in the flour.

4 Evenly divide the apple and kumquat mixture among the prepared moulds. Top with the sponge mixture. Cover the moulds and place in the steamer. Steam for 45 minutes.

5 Meanwhile, make the sauce. Place the kumquats, sugar and water in a pan and bring to the boil, stirring to dissolve the sugar. Simmer gently for 5 minutes.

6 Stir in the crème fraîche and bring back to the boil, stirring. Remove the pan from the heat and gradually whisk in the cornflour mixture. Simmer very gently for 2 minutes, stirring constantly. Add lemon juice to taste. Turn out the puddings and serve hot, with the sauce.

Per portion Energy 402kcal/1680kJ; Protein 3.7g; Carbohydrate 44.4g, of which sugars 33.7g; Fat 24.5g, of which saturates 15.3g; Cholesterol 109mg; Calcium 93mg; Fibre 1g; Sodium 190mg.

CAKES AND BAKING

The addition of apples in baking gives a wonderfully sweet, moist texture to a host of home-baked treats. From crunchy, crumbly cookies and sharp, spongy muffins to spicy cakes and juicy pastries, there is something to suit all tastes and occasions.

Apple crumble and custard slices

These luscious apple slices are easy to make using ready-made sweet pastry and custard. Just think, all the ingredients of one of the world's most popular desserts – in a cookie.

Makes 16
350g/12oz ready-made sweet pastry
1 large cooking apple, about 250g/9oz
30ml/2 tbsp caster (superfine) sugar
60ml/4 tbsp ready-made thick custard

For the crumble topping
115g/4oz/1 cup plain (all-purpose) flour
2.5ml/½ tsp ground cinnamon
60ml/4 tbsp sugar
90g/3½oz/7 tbsp unsalted butter, melted

1 Preheat the oven to 190°C/375°F/ Gas 5. Roll out the pastry and use to line the base of a 28 × 18cm/11 × 7in shallow cake tin (pan). Prick the pastry with a fork, line with foil and baking beans and bake blind for about 10–15 minutes.

2 Remove the foil and baking beans and return the pastry to the oven for a further 5 minutes until cooked and golden brown.

> **Cook's tip**
> For best results, buy the best quality custard you can find.

3 Meanwhile, peel, core and chop the apple evenly. Place in a pan with the sugar. Heat gently until the sugar dissolves, then cover with a lid and cook gently for 5–7 minutes until a thick purée is formed. Beat with a wooden spoon and set aside to cool.

4 Mix the cold apple with the custard. Spread over the pastry. To make the crumble topping, put the flour, cinnamon and sugar into a bowl and pour over the melted butter. Stir thoroughly until the mixture forms small clumps. Sprinkle the crumble over the filling.

5 Return to the oven and bake for about 10–15 minutes until the crumble topping is cooked and a golden brown. Leave to cool in the tin, then slice into bars to serve.

Per portion Energy 196kcal/822kJ; Protein 2.1g; Carbohydrate 23.7g, of which sugars 8.1g; Fat 11g, of which saturates 4.9g; Cholesterol 15mg; Calcium 37mg; Fibre 0.9g; Sodium 124mg.

Toffee apple and oat crunchies

An unashamedly addictive mixture of chewy oats, soft apple and wonderfully crunchy toffee, this cookie won't win large prizes in the looks department but is top of the class for flavour.

Makes about 16
150g/5oz/10 tbsp unsalted butter
175g/6oz/¾ cup light muscovado
  (brown) sugar
90g/3½oz/½ cup white sugar
1 large (US extra large) egg, beaten
75g/3oz/⅔ cup plain (all-purpose) flour
2.5ml/½ tsp bicarbonate of soda
  (baking soda)
a pinch of salt
250g/9oz/2½ cups rolled oats
50g/2oz/scant ½ cup sultanas
  (golden raisins)
50g/2oz dried apple rings,
  coarsely chopped
50g/2oz chewy toffees,
  coarsely chopped

1 Preheat the oven to 180°C/350°F/ Gas 4. Line two or three baking sheets with baking parchment. Beat together the butter and both sugars until creamy. Add the beaten egg and stir well until thoroughly combined.

2 Sift together the flour, bicarbonate of soda and salt. Add to the egg mixture and mix in well. Finally add the oats, sultanas, chopped apple rings and toffee and stir until just combined.

Variation
Ripe, juicy pears will also work very well in this recipe.

3 Using a small ice cream scoop or large tablespoon, place heaps of the mixture well apart on the prepared baking sheets. Bake for about 10–12 minutes, or until lightly set in the centre and just beginning to brown at the edges.

4 Remove from the oven and leave to cool on the baking sheets for a few minutes. Using a palette knife or metal spatula, transfer the cookies to a wire rack to cool completely.

Per portion Energy 249kcal/1047kJ; Protein 3.1g; Carbohydrate 38.8g, of which sugars 23.2g; Fat 10.1g, of which saturates 5.3g; Cholesterol 32mg; Calcium 34mg; Fibre 1.3g; Sodium 79mg.

Apple and elderflower stars

These delicious, crumbly apple cookies are topped with a sweet yet very sharp icing. Packaged in a pretty box, they would make a delightfully festive gift for someone special.

Makes 18
115g/4oz/½ cup unsalted butter, at room
   temperature, diced
75g/3oz/scant ½ cup caster (superfine)
   sugar
2.5ml/½ tsp mixed (apple pie) spice
1 large (US extra large) egg yolk
25g/1oz dried apple rings,
   finely chopped
200g/7oz/1¾ cups self-raising
   (self-rising) flour
5–10ml/1–2 tsp milk, if necessary

For the topping
200g/7oz/1¾ cups icing (confectioners')
   sugar, sifted
60–90ml/4–6 tbsp elderflower cordial
sugar, for sprinkling

1 Preheat the oven to 190°C/375°F/ Gas 5.

2 Cream together the butter and sugar until light and fluffy. Beat in the mixed spice and egg yolk.

3 Add the chopped apple and flour and stir together well. The mixture should form a stiff dough but if it is too dry, add some milk.

4 Roll the dough out on a floured surface to 5mm/¼in thick. Draw a five-pointed star on cardboard. Cut out and use as a template for the cookies. Alternatively, use a star biscuit (cookie) cutter.

5 Place the cookies on non-stick baking sheets and bake for about 10–15 minutes, or until just beginning to brown around the edges.

6 Using a palette knife or metal spatula, carefully transfer the cookies to a wire rack to cool.

7 To make the topping, sift the icing sugar into a bowl and add just enough elderflower cordial to mix to a fairly thick but still pourable consistency.

Cook's tip
Try to buy the darker dried apple rings as these have no added preservatives.

8 When the cookies are completely cool, trickle the icing randomly over the stars. Immediately sprinkle with sugar and leave to set.

Per portion Energy 157kcal/659kJ; Protein 1.4g; Carbohydrate 26.6g, of which sugars 18.1g; Fat 5.7g, of which saturates 3.4g; Cholesterol 25mg; Calcium 27mg; Fibre 0.4g; Sodium 42mg.

Apple and cranberry muffins

Sweet, sharp and moreish, these spiced muffins are packed with of fruit.

Makes 12
1 egg
50g/2oz/¼ cup butter, melted
100g/4oz/generous ½ cup caster
 (superfine) sugar
grated rind of 1 large orange
120ml/4fl oz/½ cup freshly squeezed
 orange juice
140g/5oz/1¼ cups plain (all-purpose) flour
5ml/1 tsp baking powder
2.5ml/½ tsp ground cinnamon
2.5ml/½ tsp freshly grated nutmeg
2.5ml/½ tsp ground allspice
a pinch of ground ginger
a pinch of salt
2 small eating apples
170g/6oz/1½ cups cranberries
55g/2oz/1⅓ cups walnuts, chopped
icing (confectioners') sugar, for dusting

Variation
Try replacing the cranberries with blackberries or blackcurrants.

---

1 Preheat the oven to 180°C/350°F/ Gas 4. Lightly grease the cups of a muffin tin (pan) or line them with paper cases.

2 In a bowl, whisk the egg with the melted butter to combine.

3 Add the sugar, grated orange rind and juice. Whisk to blend. Set aside.

4 In a large bowl, sift together the flour, baking powder, cinnamon, nutmeg, allspice, ginger and salt.

5 Make a well in the dry ingredients and pour in the egg mixture. With a spoon, stir until just blended.

6 Peel, core and quarter the apples. Chop the apple flesh coarsely with a sharp knife.

7 Add the apples, cranberries and walnuts to the batter and stir lightly to blend.

8 Three-quarters fill the cups. Bake for 25–30 minutes, until golden. Leave to stand for 5 minutes before transferring to a wire rack to cool. Dust with icing sugar before serving. Store in an airtight container for up to 3 days.

Per portion Energy 149kcal/624kJ; Protein 2.5g; Carbohydrate 20.4g, of which sugars 10.8g; Fat 6.9g, of which saturates 2.6g; Cholesterol 25mg; Calcium 30mg; Fibre 0.9g; Sodium 34mg.

Apple and cinnamon cake

Moist and spicy, this is perfect for packed lunches or afternoon tea.

Makes a 20cm/8in square cake
115g/4oz/½ cup low-fat spread
200g/7oz/1¼ cups dried, stoned dates
1–2 tart eating apples or 1 cooking apple, about 225g/8oz, peeled and grated
7.5ml/1½ tsp mixed (apple pie) spice
5ml/1 tsp ground cinnamon
2.5ml/½ tsp salt
75g/3oz/½ cup raisins
2 eggs, beaten
150g/5oz/1¼ cups wholemeal (whole-wheat) flour, sifted
115g/4oz/generous 1 cup gram flour, sifted with 10ml/2 tsp baking powder
175ml/6fl oz/¾ cup unsweetened coconut milk

1 Preheat the oven to 180°C/350°F/Gas 4. Grease a deep 20cm/8in square baking tin (pan) and line the base. Blend the spread and the dates. Add the apple, mixed spice, cinnamon and salt. Process until blended.

2 Scrape the apple and date mixture into a bowl and fold in the raisins and beaten eggs alternately with the flours, baking powder and coconut milk. Transfer to the prepared tin.

3 Bake for 30–40 minutes until dark golden and firm to the touch. Cool the cake in the tin for 15 minutes before turning out on a wire rack to cool completely.

Per cake: Energy 2036kcal/8588kJ; Carbohydrate 300g; sugar total150g; Fat, total 72g; saturated fat 4.5g; polyunsaturated fat 18.5g; monounsaturated fat 28g; starch 147g; Fibre 34.4g; Sodium 2412mg.

Apple and sour cream crumble muffins

One-third of the cooking apples in this recipe are sliced and coated in a sweet almond crumble, which makes a delicious crunchy texture for the muffin top.

Makes 8
3 cooking apples, peeled and cored
115g/4oz/generous ½ cup caster (superfine) sugar, plus 10ml/2 tsp for coating
5ml/1 tsp ground cinnamon
250g/9oz/2¼ cups plain (all-purpose) flour
15ml/1 tbsp baking powder
75g/3oz/6 tbsp butter, melted
2 eggs, beaten
30ml/2 tbsp sour cream

For the cinnamon crumble
30ml/2 tbsp plain (all-purpose) flour
45ml/3 tbsp demerara (raw) sugar
30ml/2 tbsp ground almonds
a pinch of ground cinnamon

1 Preheat the oven to 190°C/375°F/Gas 5. Line the cups of a muffin tin (pan) with paper cases.

2 To make the crumble, combine all of the crumble ingredients together in a mixing bowl.

3 Cut one apple into thin crescents, and toss in the crumble. Set aside.

4 Dice the remaining apples. Sift 10ml/2 tsp sugar and the cinnamon over the top. Set aside.

5 Sift the flour, baking powder and sugar into a bowl. Stir in the melted butter, eggs and sour cream. Add the apple chunks and lightly fold them into the mixture.

6 Fill the cases with the mixture, then arrange the crumble-coated apple on top. Bake for 25 minutes until risen and golden. Cool on a wire rack. Store for up to three days.

Per portion Energy 272kcal/1144kJ; Protein 4.8g; Carbohydrate 42.8g, of which sugars 19g; Fat 10.2g, of which saturates 6g; Cholesterol 71mg; Calcium 65mg; Fibre 1.6g; Sodium 92mg.

Spicy apple cake

This moist and spicy apple cake comes from Germany where it can be found on the menu of coffee and tea houses.

Serves 12

115g/4oz/1 cup plain (all-purpose) flour
115g/4oz/1 cup wholemeal (whole-wheat) flour
10ml/2 tsp baking powder
5ml/1 tsp cinnamon
2.5ml/½ tsp mixed (apple pie) spice
225g/8oz cooking apple, cored, peeled and chopped
75g/3oz/6 tbsp butter
175g/6oz/generous ¾ cup soft light brown sugar
finely grated rind of 1 small orange
2 eggs, beaten
30ml/2 tbsp milk
whipped cream and cinnamon, to serve

For the topping

4 eating apples, cored and thinly sliced
juice of ½ orange
10ml/2 tsp caster sugar
45ml/3 tbsp apricot jam, warmed and sieved (strained)

1 Preheat the oven to 180°C/350°F/Gas 4.

2 Grease and line a 23cm/9in round loose-bottomed cake tin (pan). Sift the flours, baking powder and spices together in a bowl.

3 Toss the chopped cooking apple in 30ml/2 tbsp of the flour mixture.

> **Variation**
> Pears would also work well in this cake as they are moist and full of flavour.

4 In a separate bowl, cream together the butter, brown sugar and orange rind until light and fluffy. Gradually beat in the eggs, and then fold in the flour mixture, the chopped apple and the milk.

5 Spoon the mixture into the cake tin and level the surface.

6 For the topping, toss the apple slices in the orange juice and set them in overlapping circles on top of the cake mixture, pressing down lightly.

7 Sprinkle the caster sugar over the top and bake for 1–1¼ hours, or until risen and firm. Cover with foil if the apples brown too much.

8 Cool in the tin for 10 minutes, then remove to a wire rack. Glaze the apples with the sieved jam. Serve with whipped cream, sprinkled with cinnamon.

Per portion Energy 587kcal/2471kJ; Protein 5.5g; Carbohydrate 92g, of which sugars 69.7g; Fat 24.5g, of which saturates 10.6g; Cholesterol 40mg; Calcium 95mg; Fibre 2.5g; Sodium 129mg.

Apple cake with vanilla cream

Dessert apples are used in this recipe as they are naturally very sweet and therefore ideally suited to this sublime cake. It can be served while still warm yet tastes just as good when cold.

Serves 6–8
115g/4½oz/½ cup plus 15g/½oz/1 tbsp
   unsalted butter
7 eating apples
30ml/2 tbsp caster
   (superfine) sugar
10ml/2 tsp ground cinnamon
200g/7oz/1 cup sugar
2 egg yolks and 3 egg whites
100g/4oz/1 cup ground almonds
grated rind and juice of ½ lemon

For the vanilla cream
250ml/8fl oz/1 cup milk
250ml/8fl oz/1 cup double
   (heavy) cream
15ml/1 tbsp sugar
1 vanilla pod (bean), split
4 egg yolks, beaten

1 Preheat the oven to 180°C/350°F/ Gas 4. Butter a 20cm/8in flan tin (pan) using 15g/½oz/1 tbsp of the butter. Peel, core and thinly slice the apples and put the slices in a bowl. Add the caster sugar and cinnamon and mix them together. Put the mixture in the prepared tin.

2 Put the remaining butter and sugar in a bowl and whisk them together until they are light and fluffy. Beat in the egg yolks, then add the ground almonds and lemon rind and juice to the mixture.

3 Whisk the egg whites until stiff then fold into the mixture. Pour the mixture over the apples in the flan tin. Bake in the oven for approximately 40 minutes until golden brown and the apples are tender.

4 Meanwhile, make the vanilla cream. Put the milk, cream, sugar and vanilla pod in a pan and heat gently. Add a little of the warm milk mixture to the egg yolks then slowly add the egg mixture to the pan and continue to heat gently, stirring all the time, until the mixture thickens. Do not allow the mixture to boil or it will curdle.

5 Remove the vanilla pod and serve the vanilla cream warm or cold, with the apple cake.

Per portion Energy 541kcal/2254kJ; Protein 7.6g; Carbohydrate 39.7g, of which sugars 39.3g; Fat 40.3g, of which saturates 20g; Cholesterol 227mg; Calcium 122mg; Fibre 2.1g; Sodium 135mg.

Potato and apple cake

Both sweet and savoury versions of this delicious Irish potato apple cake exist. The sweet one, here, was the high point of many a traditional farmhouse high tea, especially when using home-grown apples in autumn.

Makes 2 farls; serves 4–6
450g/1lb freshly boiled potatoes
   in their skins, preferably still warm
a pinch of salt
25g/1oz/2 tbsp butter, melted
about 115g/4oz/1 cup plain
   (all-purpose) flour

For the filling
3 large or 4 small cooking apples,
   such as Bramley's Seedling
a little lemon juice (optional)
about 50g/2oz/¼ cup butter in thin slices
50–115g/2–4oz/¼ – generous ½ cup
   caster (superfine) sugar, or to taste

1 Preheat the oven to 200°C/400°F/ Gas 6. Peel the potatoes and mash them in a large heavy pan until very smooth. Season to taste with the salt, and drizzle the melted butter over.

2 Knead in as much plain flour as necessary to make a pliable dough (waxy potatoes will need more flour than naturally floury ones, such as Kerr's Pink). The dough should be elastic enough to roll out, but do not knead more than necessary.

3 Roll the potato mixture out into a large circle and cut into four farls (triangular pieces).

4 To make the filling, peel, core and slice the apples and pile the slices of the raw apple on to two of the farls. Sprinkle with a little lemon juice, if you like. Dampen the edges of the farls, place the other two on top, and nip with your fingers around the edges to seal them together.

5 Cook in the preheated oven for about 15–20 minutes (when the cake is nicely browned, the apples should be cooked).

6 Slit each cake around the side and turn the top back. Lay thin slices of butter over the apples, until they are almost covered, and then sweeten with sugar. Replace the top and return to the oven for 2 minutes until the butter and sugar have melted to make a sauce.

7 Cut each farl into pieces and serve, pouring a little of the sugary butter sauce on the side.

Per farl Energy 786kcal/3307kJ; Protein 9.5g; Carbohydrate 121.9g, of which sugars 40.5g; Fat 32.4g, of which saturates 19.9g; Cholesterol 80mg; Calcium 117mg; Fibre 6.1g; Sodium 253mg.

Caramelized apple tart

The beauty of this sweet, caramelized apple tart is that it is made and baked in one pan. Although prepared upside down, when ready to serve, the pastry sits on the bottom with the caramel-coated apples on the top. This tart is delicious served with either cream or custard.

Serves 4
200g/7oz/scant 1 cup butter
200g/7oz/1 cup caster (superfine) sugar
6 large eating apples

For the sweet pastry
150g/5oz/10 tbsp butter
50g/2oz/¼ cup caster (superfine) sugar
225g/8oz/2 cups plain (all-purpose) flour
1 egg

1 Make the sweet pastry. Cream the butter with the caster sugar together in a food processor. Add the plain flour and egg. Mix until just combined, being careful not to overprocess. Cover and leave in a cool place for an hour before use.

2 Preheat the oven to 200°C/400°F/ Gas 6. For the filling, cut the butter into small pieces. Using a shallow, 30cm/12in ovenproof frying pan, heat the sugar and butter and allow to caramelize over a low heat, stirring continuously for about 10 minutes.

3 Meanwhile peel and core the apples then cut them into eighths. When the butter and sugar are caramelized, place the apples in the pan in a circular fan, one layer around the outside then one in the centre. The pan should be full. Reduce the heat and cook for 5 minutes, then remove from the heat.

4 Roll out the pastry to a circle big enough to fit the pan completely with generous edgings. Spread the pastry over the fruit and tuck in the edges. Bake in the oven for about 30 minutes, or until the pastry is browned and set. Remove from the oven and leave to rest.

5 When ready to serve, gently reheat the tart on the stove for a few minutes then invert on to a warmed serving plate, so the pastry forms the base.

Per portion Energy 904kcal/3774kJ; Protein 4.6g; Carbohydrate 95.2g, of which sugars 66.5g; Fat 58.8g, of which saturates 31.5g; Cholesterol 116mg; Calcium 95mg; Fibre 3.6g; Sodium 559mg.

Deep-dish apple pie

This all-time classic favourite is made with rich shortcrust pastry. Inside, sugar, spices and flour create a deliciously thick and syrupy sauce with the apple juices.

Serves 6
115g/4oz/generous ½ cup caster
   (superfine) sugar
45ml/3 tbsp plain (all-purpose) flour
2.5ml/½ tsp ground cinnamon
finely grated rind of 1 orange
900g/2lb tart cooking apples
1 egg white, lightly beaten
30ml/2 tbsp golden granulated sugar
whipped cream, to serve

For the pastry
350g/12oz/3 cups plain
   (all-purpose) flour
a pinch of salt
175g/6oz/¾ cup butter, diced
about 75ml/5 tbsp chilled water

1 To make the pastry, sift the flour and salt into a mixing bowl and rub or cut in the butter until the mixture resembles fine breadcrumbs.

2 Sprinkle over the water and mix to a dough. Knead lightly for a few seconds until smooth. Wrap the dough in clear film (plastic wrap) and chill for 30 minutes.

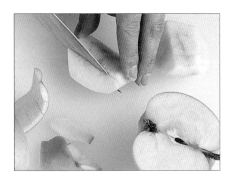

3 Combine the caster sugar, flour, cinnamon and orange rind in a bowl. Peel, core and thinly slice the apples. Add to the sugar mixture, then toss gently until they are all evenly coated.

4 Put a baking sheet in the oven and preheat to 200°C/400°F/Gas 6. Roll out just over half the pastry and use to line a 23cm/9in pie dish that is 4cm/1½in deep, allowing the pastry to overhang the edges slightly.

5 Spoon in the filling, doming the apple slices in the centre.

6 Roll out the remaining pastry to form the lid. Lightly brush the edges of the pastry case with a little water, then carefully place the lid over the apple filling.

7 Trim the pastry with a sharp knife. Gently press the edges together to seal, then knock up the edge. Re-roll the pastry trimmings and cut out apple and leaf shapes. Brush the top of the pie with egg white. Arrange the pastry apples and leaves on top.

8 Brush again with egg white, then sprinkle with golden granulated sugar. Make two small slits in the top of the pie to allow steam to escape.

9 Bake for 30 minutes, then lower the oven temperature to 180°C/350°F/Gas 4 and bake for a further 15 minutes until the pastry is golden and the apples are soft – check by inserting a small sharp knife or skewer through one of the slits in the top of the pie. Serve hot, with whipped cream.

Per portion Energy 591kcal/2488kJ; Protein 7.4g; Carbohydrate 89.9g, of which sugars 39.8g; Fat 25g, of which saturates 15.3g; Cholesterol 62mg; Calcium 117mg; Fibre 4.4g; Sodium 193mg.

Blueberry and apple pie

The traditional wild harvest of blueberries (also known as bilberries, whinberries or whortleberries) has always been gathered with great excitement. These berries are popular pie fillings and a good accompaniment to apples.

Serves 6

2 cooking apples, total weight
  about 400g/14oz
10ml/2 tsp cornflour (cornstarch)
350g/12oz/3 cups whinberries
40–50g/3–4 tbsp caster (superfine)
  sugar, plus extra for sprinkling
milk, for brushing

For the pastry

250g/9oz/2¼ cups plain
  (all-purpose) flour
25g/1oz/2 tbsp caster
  (superfine) sugar
150g/5oz/10 tbsp butter, chilled
  and cut into small cubes
1 egg

Cook's tip

Whinberries give out a lot of juice, so avoid using a loose-bottomed tin (pan) in case it leaks out on to the oven floor.

1 Sift the flour into a bowl and stir in the sugar. Add the butter and rub into the flour until the mixture resembles fine crumbs.

2 Stir in the egg and enough cold water until the mixture forms clumps, then gather it together to make a smooth dough. Wrap the pastry in clear film (plastic wrap) and place in the refrigerator for 20–30 minutes.

3 Preheat the oven to 190°C/375°F/ Gas 5.

4 On a lightly floured surface, roll out half the dough to make a circle large enough to line a deep 23cm/9in ovenproof dish or tart tin (pan). Gently press the pastry into the corners of the dish and ensure that the pastry hangs over the sides slightly.

5 Roll out the remaining pastry to a circle large enough to make a lid and check it for size.

6 Peel the apples, remove their cores and chop them into small pieces. Toss the apple pieces with the cornflour until evenly coated and arrange them in the bottom of the pastry case. Scatter the whinberries on top and sprinkle the sugar over. Lightly brush the edges of the pastry with water.

7 Lay the pastry lid over the fruit filling. Trim off the excess pastry and pinch the edges together to seal them well. Make a small slit in the centre to allow the steam to escape, then brush the top with milk and sprinkle with a little sugar.

8 Put the pie into the hot oven and cook for approximately 30–40 minutes until the pastry is crisp and golden brown and the filling is cooked through. While the pie is still hot, sprinkle with more caster sugar and serve with a dollop of ice cream or piping hot custard.

Per portion Energy 403kcal/1688kJ; Protein 5.76g; Carbohydrate 51.4g, of which sugars 18.15g; Fat 20.8g, of which saturates 12.5g; Cholesterol 81.5mg; Calcium 98.6mg; Fibre 3,5g; Sodium 157.5mg.

Crunchy apple and almond flan

Do not be tempted to put any sugar with the apples, as this makes them produce too much liquid. All of the sweetness is in the pastry and the crunchy topping.

Serves 8
115g/4oz/1 cup plain (all-purpose) flour
1.5ml/¼ tsp mixed (apple pie) spice
50g/2oz/¼ cup butter, diced
50g/2oz/¼ cup demerara (raw) sugar
50g/2oz/½ cup flaked (sliced) almonds
675g/1½lb cooking apples
25g/1oz/3 tbsp raisins
icing (confectioners') sugar, for dusting

For the pastry
175g/6oz/1½ cups plain
  (all-purpose) flour
75g/3oz/6 tbsp butter, diced
25g/1oz/¼ cup ground almonds
25g/1oz/2 tbsp caster (superfine) sugar
1 egg yolk
15ml/1 tbsp cold water
1.5ml/¼ tsp almond extract

2 Meanwhile, make the topping. Sift the flour and mixed spice into a mixing bowl and rub in the butter with your fingertips. Stir in the demerara sugar and flaked almonds.

3 Roll out the pastry on a lightly floured work surface and use to line a 23cm/9in loose-based flan tin (quiche pan), taking care to press the pastry neatly into the edges and to make a lip around the top edge. Use a rolling pin to trim off the excess pastry and give a neat edge. Chill the pastry flan for 15 minutes.

4 Place a baking sheet in the oven and preheat to 190°C/375°F/Gas 5.

5 Peel, core and thinly slice the cooking apples. Arrange the slices in the pastry case in overlapping, concentric circles, creating a dome of apples in the centre. Sprinkle over the raisins.

6 Cover the apples with the crunchy topping mixture, pressing it on lightly. Place the flan on the hot baking sheet and bake for 25–30 minutes, or until the top is golden brown and the apples are tender (you can test them with a fine skewer). Leave the flan to cool in the tin for 10 minutes. Serve warm or cold, with a generous dusting of sifted icing sugar.

Per portion Energy 358kcal/1499kJ; Protein 6.2g; Carbohydrate 42.5g, of which sugars 14.6g; Fat 19.3g, of which saturates 8.8g; Cholesterol 59mg; Calcium 86mg; Fibre 3.2g; Sodium 102mg.

1 For the pastry, place the flour in a food processor or mixing bowl and rub in the butter until the mixture resembles fine breadcrumbs. Stir in the ground almonds and sugar. Whisk the egg yolk, water and almond extract together and mix into the dry ingredients to form a dough. Knead until smooth, wrap in clear film (plastic wrap) and leave in a cool place for 20 minutes.

Cook's tip
Don't worry if the pie seems too full after adding the apple slices; as the apples cook the filling will drop slightly.

Apple turnovers

These fruity pastry parcels are always popular, and since they are baked in the oven, are a slightly healthier option than fritters fried in oil.

Makes 12

250g/9oz/2¼ cups plain (all-purpose) flour, plus extra for dusting
2.5ml/½ tsp salt
90g/3½oz/scant ½ cup cold butter
5ml/1 tsp white wine vinegar
500g/1¼lb tart apples, such as Goudrenet or Granny Smith
45ml/3 tbsp soft brown sugar
5ml/1 tsp ground cinnamon
2.5ml/½ tsp crushed fennel seeds
beaten egg, to glaze
icing (confectioner's) sugar, for sprinkling

1 Sift the flour and salt into a bowl, coarsely grate in the butter and rub in with your fingertips. Using the blade of a knife, gradually stir in 100ml/3½fl oz/scant ½ cup water and the vinegar. Gather the dough together and shape into a ball.

2 Roll out the dough on a lightly floured surface, then fold the top edge down to the centre and the bottom edge up to the centre and roll out again to a rectangle.

3 Fold in three again, cover with clear film (plastic wrap) and leave to rest in the refrigerator.

4 Peel the apples and grate coarsely into a bowl. Stir in the sugar, cinnamon and fennel seeds.

5 Preheat the oven to 200°C/400°F/Gas 6. Line a 30 × 40cm/12 × 16in baking sheet with baking parchment.

6 Roll out the dough on a lightly floured surface to 36 × 48cm/14¼ × 19in rectangle, then cut into 12 squares. Cover the centre of each with some grated apple and fold over into a triangle. Press the edges together.

7 Transfer to the prepared baking sheet and brush with beaten egg. Prick the tops several times with a fork. Bake for about 35 minutes, until golden. Remove from the oven and leave to cool, then sprinkle with icing sugar.

Per item Energy 156kcal/658kJ; Protein 2.2g; Carbohydrate 23.9g, of which sugars 8g; Fat 6.5g, of which saturates 4g; Cholesterol 16mg; Calcium 34mg; Fibre 1.3g; Sodium 47mg.

Apple strudel

This classic recipe is usually made with strudel dough, but filo pastry makes a good shortcut.

Serves 4–6
75g/3oz/¾ cup hazelnuts, chopped
   and roasted
30ml/2 tbsp nibbed almonds, roasted
50g/2oz/4 tbsp demerara (raw) sugar
2.5ml/½ tsp ground cinnamon
grated rind and juice of ½ lemon
2 large cooking apples, peeled,
   cored and chopped
50g/2oz/⅓ cup sultanas (golden raisins)
4 large sheets filo pastry, thawed
   if frozen
50g/2oz/4 tbsp unsalted butter, melted
icing (confectioners') sugar,
   for dredging

1 Preheat the oven to 190°C/375°F/ Gas 5. In a bowl mix together the hazelnuts, almonds, sugar, cinnamon, lemon rind and juice, apples and sultanas. Set aside.

2 Lay one sheet of filo pastry on a floured surface and brush with melted butter. Lay a second sheet on top and brush again with melted butter. Repeat with the remaining two sheets.

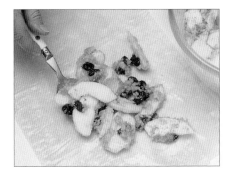

3 Put the apple filling on the pastry, with a 2.5cm/1in border all around.

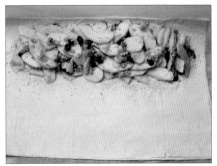

4 Fold in the two shorter sides to enclose the filling, then roll up like a Swiss (jelly) roll. Place on a lightly buttered baking sheet seam side down.

Cook's tip
Keep the filo sheets covered with a damp dish towel as you work.

5 Brush the pastry with the remaining butter. Bake for 30–40 minutes or until golden brown. Leave to cool before dusting generously with icing sugar. Serve the strudel warm or cold in thick diagonal slices.

Per portion Energy 287kcal/1199kJ; Protein 4.4g; Carbohydrate 29.1g, of which sugars 19.2g; Fat 17.8g, of which saturates 5.2g; Cholesterol 18mg; Calcium 60mg; Fibre 2.4g; Sodium 55mg.

PRESERVES

Preserving seasonal fruits and vegetables was once essential for survival and is one of the oldest of culinary arts. From tart to sweet, the range of apple flavours makes them a perfect addition to preserves such as jams, jellies, marmalades, sauces and chutneys, even spiced 'butter' and mincemeat.

Blackberry and apple cheese

This rich, dark preserve has an incredibly intense flavour.

Makes about 900g/2lb
900g/2lb/8 cups blackberries
450g/1lb tart cooking apples,
   cut into chunks, with skins
   and cores included
grated rind and juice of 1 lemon
800g/1¾lb/4 cups sugar, warmed

1 Put the blackberries, apples and lemon rind and juice in a pan and pour in enough water to come halfway up the fruit. Bring to the boil, then simmer uncovered for 15–20 minutes.

2 Leave the fruit to cool slightly, then turn into a sieve (strainer) and press into a bowl, using the back of a spoon. Measure the purée into a large, heavy pan, adding 400g/14oz/ 2 cups warmed sugar for every 600ml/1 pint/2½ cups purée.

3 Gently heat the purée, stirring, until the sugar dissolves. Increase the heat slightly and cook for 40–50 minutes, stirring frequently, until very thick.

4 Spoon the cheese into warmed, sterilized straight-sided jars or oiled moulds. Seal and label the jars or moulds. Store them in a cool, dark place for 2–3 months to dry out slightly.

> **Cook's tip**
> When the cheese is ready, you should be able to see the base of the pan when a wooden spoon is drawn through the mixture. Spoon a small amount of the mixture on to a chilled plate; it should form a firm jelly.

Per 900g/2lb Energy 3534kcal/15064kJ; Protein 13.5g; Carbohydrate 921.9g, of which sugars 921.9g; Fat 2.3g, of which saturates 0g; Cholesterol 0mg; Calcium 811mg; Fibre 35.1g; Sodium 75mg.

Apple sauce

Really more of a condiment than a sauce, this tart purée is usually served cold or warm, rather than hot. It is traditional with roast pork or duck, but it is also good with sausages, burgers, cold meats, pork pies, hot or cold meatloaf or cheese.

Serves 6
225g/8oz cooking apples
30ml/2 tbsp water
a thin strip of lemon rind
15g/½ oz/1 tbsp butter
15–30ml/1–2 tbsp sugar

1 Peel the apples, cut into quarters and remove the cores. Dice or thinly slice the apple quarters.

2 Place the apples in a pan with the water and lemon rind. Cook, uncovered, over a low heat until very soft, stirring occasionally.

3 Remove the lemon rind from the pan and discard. Beat the apples to a pulp with a spoon.

4 Stir in the butter, then add sugar to taste. Transfer to a serving dish, cover and leave to cool before serving.

Per portion Energy 60kcal/251kJ; Protein 0.2g; Carbohydrate 6g, of which sugars 6g; Fat 4.1g, of which saturates 2.7g; Cholesterol 11mg; Calcium 4mg; Fibre 0.6g; Sodium 35mg.

Rosehip and apple jelly

This economical jelly is made with windfall apples and wild rosehips. It is rich in vitamin C and full of flavour.

Makes about 2kg/4½lb
1kg/2¼lb windfall cooking apples, peeled, trimmed and quartered
450g/1lb firm, ripe rosehips
about 1.3kg/3lb/6½ cups sugar, warmed

1 Place the quartered apples in a large pan with just enough water to cover, plus 300ml/½ pint/1¼ cups of extra water. Bring the mixture to the boil and cook gently until the apples soften and turn to a pulp.

2 Chop the rosehips coarsely. Add them to the pan with the apple and simmer for a further 10 minutes.

3 Remove from the heat and leave to stand for 10 minutes. Pour the mixture into a scalded jelly bag suspended over a non-metallic bowl. Leave to drain overnight.

4 Measure the juice into a preserving pan and bring to the boil. Add 400g/14oz/2 cups warmed sugar for each 600ml/1 pint/2½ cups of liquid. Stir until the sugar has completely dissolved. Boil, without stirring, for 10 minutes, or until the jelly reaches setting point (105°C/220°F).

5 Pour the jelly into warmed, sterilized jars and seal. Label and store when completely cold.

Per 2kg/4½lb Energy 5684kcal/24,259kJ; Protein 8.4g; Carbohydrate 1505.7g, of which sugars 1505.7g; Fat 0.5g, of which saturates 0g; Cholesterol 0mg; Calcium 761mg; Fibre 7.7g; Sodium 94mg.

Rowan and crab apple jelly

This astringent jelly is made from the orange fruit of mountain ash trees. It is a traditional accompaniment to game, especially venison.

Makes about 2.25kg/5lb
1.3kg/3lb/12 cups rowan berries
450g/1lb crab apples, or windfall cooking apples
450g/1lb/2¼ cups sugar per 600ml/ 1 pint/2½ cups juice, warmed

1 Cut the rowan berries off their stalks, rinse them in a colander and put them into a preserving pan.

2 Remove any badly damaged parts from the apples before weighing them, then cut them up roughly without peeling or coring. Add the apples to the pan, with 1.2 litres/2 pints/5 cups water, which should just cover the fruit.

3 Bring to the boil and simmer for about 45 minutes, until the fruit is soft, stirring occasionally and crushing the fruit with a wooden spoon to help extract the pectin. Strain the fruit through a scalded jelly bag or a fine sieve into a bowl overnight.

4 Measure the juice and allow 450g/1lb/2¼ cups sugar per 600ml/ 1 pint/2½ cups juice. Return the juice to the rinsed preserving pan and add the measured amount of sugar.

5 Stir over a low heat until the sugar has dissolved, and then bring to the boil and boil hard for about 10 minutes until setting point is reached. To test, put a spoonful of jam on to a cold saucer.

6 Allow to cool slightly, and then push the surface of the jam with your finger. Setting point has been reached if a skin has formed. If not, boil a little longer and keep testing until it sets.

7 Skim, if necessary, and pour into warmed, sterilized jars. Cover, seal and store in a cool, dark place until needed. The jelly will store well for 6 months.

Per 2.25kg/5lb Energy 2340kcal/9993kJ; Protein 15.8g; Carbohydrate 606.4g, of which sugars 606.4g; Fat 0.5g, of which saturates 0g; Cholesterol 0mg; Calcium 1.03g; Fibre 54g; Sodium 80mg.

Spiced cider and apple jelly

This wonderful spicy jelly has a rich, warming flavour, making it ideal to serve during the cold winter months. Serve as a spread or use it to sweeten apple pies and desserts.

Makes about 1.3kg/3lb
900g/2lb tart cooking apples, coarsely chopped with skins and cores included
900ml/1¼ pints/3¾ cups sweet (hard) cider
juice and pips (seeds) of 2 oranges
1 cinnamon stick
6 whole cloves
150ml/¼ pint/⅔ cup water
about 900g/2lb/4½ cups sugar, warmed

1 Put the apples, cider, juice and pips, cinnamon, cloves and water in a large pan. Bring to the boil, cover and simmer for about 1 hour.

2 Leave to cool slightly, then pour the fruit into a scalded jelly bag suspended over a non-metallic bowl and leave to drain overnight.

Cook's tip
There is no need to remove all the peel from the apples: simply cut out any bruised, damaged or bad areas.

3 Measure the strained juice into a preserving pan. Add 450g/1lb/2¼ cups warmed sugar for every 600ml/1 pint/ 2½ cups juice.

4 Heat, stirring, over a low heat until the sugar has dissolved. Increase the heat and boil, without stirring, for 10 minutes, or until the jelly reaches setting point (105°C/220°F).

5 Remove from the heat and skim off any scum. Ladle into warmed sterilized jars. Cover, seal and label.

Per 1.3kg/3lb Energy 3975kcal/16,950kJ; Protein 5.4g; Carbohydrate 990.6g, of which sugars 990.6g; Fat 0.3g, of which saturates 0g; Cholesterol 0mg; Calcium 561mg; Fibre 4.8g; Sodium 123mg.

Apple and cinnamon butter

Fans of apple pies and crumbles will love this luscious apple butter.

Makes about 1.8kg/4lb
475ml/16fl oz/2 cups dry (hard) cider
450g/1lb tart cooking apples,
    peeled, cored and sliced
450g/1lb eating apples, peeled,
    cored and sliced
grated rind and juice of 1 lemon
675g/1½lb/scant 3½ cups sugar,
    warmed
5ml/1 tsp ground cinnamon

1 Pour the cider into a large pan and bring to the boil. Boil hard until the volume is reduced by half, then add the apples and lemon rind and juice. Cover the pan. Cook for 10 minutes. Uncover and cook for 20–30 minutes.

2 Leave the mixture to cool slightly, then blend to a purée. Press through a fine sieve (strainer) into a bowl.

3 Measure the purée into a large, heavy pan, adding 275g/10oz/1⅓ cups warmed sugar for every 600ml/1 pint/ 2½ cups of purée. Add the ground cinnamon and stir well to combine.

4 Gently heat the mixture, stirring continuously, until the sugar dissolves. Increase the heat and boil steadily for 20 minutes, stirring frequently, until it forms a thick purée. Spoon the butter into warmed sterilized jars. Seal and label, then store in a cool, dark place for 2 days.

Per 1.8kg/4lb Energy 3145kcal/13,428kJ; Protein 6.1g; Carbohydrate 797.8g, of which sugars 797.8g; Fat 0.9g, of which saturates 0g; Cholesterol 0mg; Calcium 432mg; Fibre 14.4g; Sodium 92mg.

Spiced apple mincemeat

This fruity mincemeat is traditionally used to fill little pies at Christmas but it is great at any time. Try it as a filling for large tarts finished with a lattice top and served with custard. To make a lighter mincemeat, add some extra grated apple just before using.

Makes about 1.8kg/4lb
500g/1¼lb tart cooking apples,
    peeled, cored and finely diced
115g/4oz/½ cup ready-to-eat dried
    apricots, coarsely chopped
900g/2lb/5⅓ cups luxury dried
    mixed fruit
115g/4oz/1 cup whole blanched
    almonds, chopped
175g/6oz/1 cup shredded beef
    or vegetarian suet (chilled,
    grated shortening)
225g/8oz/1 cup dark muscovado
    (molasses) sugar
grated rind and juice of 1 orange
grated rind and juice of 1 lemon
5ml/1 tsp ground cinnamon
2.5ml/½ tsp freshly grated nutmeg
2.5ml/½ tsp ground ginger
120ml/4fl oz/½ cup brandy

1 Put the apples, apricots, dried fruit, almonds, suet and sugar in a large non-metallic bowl and stir together until thoroughly combined.

2 Add the orange and lemon rind and juice, cinnamon, nutmeg, ginger and brandy and mix well.

3 Cover the bowl with a clean dish towel and leave to stand in a cool place for 2 days, stirring occasionally.

4 Spoon the mincemeat into cool sterilized jars, pressing down well, and being very careful not to trap any air bubbles. Cover and seal.

5 Store the jars in a cool, dark place for at least 4 weeks before using.

6 Once opened, store in the refrigerator and use within 4 weeks. Unopened, the mincemeat will keep for 1 year.

Per 1.8kg/4lb Energy 6071kcal/25,579kJ; Protein 52.2g; Carbohydrate 963.6g, of which sugars 939.7g; Fat 227.3g, of which saturates 92.4g; Cholesterol 144mg; Calcium 1156mg; Fibre 44.4g; Sodium 488mg.

Apple and tomato chutney

This mellow, golden, spicy chutney makes the most of fresh autumn produce. Any type of organic tomatoes can be used successfully in this recipe.

Makes about 1.8kg/4lb
1.3kg/3lb cooking apples
1.3kg/3lb tomatoes
2 large onions
2 garlic cloves
250g/9oz/1¾ cups pitted dates
2 red (bell) peppers
3 dried red chillies
15ml/1 tbsp black peppercorns
4 cardamom pods
15ml/1 tbsp coriander seeds
10ml/2 tsp cumin seeds
10ml/2 tsp ground turmeric
5ml/1 tsp salt
600ml/1 pint/2½ cups distilled
    malt vinegar
1kg/2¼lb/5¼ cups unrefined sugar
    or rapadura

1 Peel and chop the apples. Peel and chop the tomatoes, onions and garlic. Quarter the dates. Core and seed the peppers, then cut into chunky pieces. Put all the prepared ingredients, except the red peppers, into a preserving pan.

2 Slit the chillies. Put the peppercorns and remaining spices into a mortar and roughly crush with a pestle. Add the chillies, spices and salt to the pan.

3 Pour in the vinegar and sugar, bring to the boil and simmer for 30 minutes, stirring occasionally. Add the red pepper and cook for a further 30 minutes, stirring more frequently as the chutney becomes thick and pulpy.

4 Spoon the chutney into warm, dry, sterilized jars. Seal each jar, label and leave to cool. Store in a cool, dry place.

Per 1.8kg/4lb Energy 5583kcal/23818kJ; Protein 35.7g; Carbohydrate 1432.9g, of which sugars 1420.3g; Fat 8.1g, of which saturates 1.9g; Cholesterol 0mg; Calcium 940mg; Fibre 56.4g; Sodium 6152mg.

Apple and red onion marmalade

This marmalade chutney is good enough to eat on its own. Serve it with good pork sausages for thoroughly modern hot dogs or in a ham sandwich instead of mustard.

Makes 450g/1lb
60ml/4 tbsp extra virgin olive oil
900g/2lb red onions, thinly sliced
75g/3oz/scant ½ cup demerara
    (raw) sugar
2 Cox's Orange Pippin apples
90ml/6 tbsp cider vinegar

1 Heat the oil in a large, heavy pan. Add the onions. Stir in the sugar and cook, uncovered, over a medium heat for 40 minutes, stirring occasionally, or until the onions have softened and become a rich golden colour.

2 Peel, core and grate the apples. Add them to the pan with the vinegar and continue to cook for 20 minutes until the chutney is thick and sticky. Spoon into a sterilized jar and cover.

3 When cool, label and store in the refrigerator for up to 1 month.

Per 450g/1lb Energy 1271kcal/5298kJ; Protein 13g; Carbohydrate 173g, of which sugars 152g; Fat 62g, of which saturates 8.6g; Cholesterol 0mg; Calcium 257mg; Fibre 16.6g; Sodium 41mg.

Kashmir chutney

In the true tradition of the Kashmiri country store, this is a typical family recipe passed down from generation to generation. It is wonderful served with plain or spicy grilled sausages.

Makes about 2.75kg/6lb
1kg/2¼lb green eating apples
15g/½oz garlic cloves
1 litre/1¾ pints/4 cups malt vinegar
450g/1lb pitted dates
115g/4oz preserved stem ginger
450g/1lb/3 cups raisins
450g/1lb/2 cups soft light brown sugar
2.5ml/½ tsp cayenne pepper
30ml/2 tbsp salt

1 Quarter the apples, remove the cores and chop coarsely, then peel and chop the garlic.

2 Place the apples and garlic in a pan with enough vinegar to cover. Bring to the boil and boil for 10 minutes.

3 Chop the dates and ginger and add them to the pan, together with the rest of the ingredients. Cook gently for 45 minutes.

4 Spoon the mixture into warmed sterilized jars and seal immediately.

> **Cook's tip**
> This sweet, chunky, spicy chutney is perfect served with cold meats for an informal buffet lunch.

Per 2.75kg/6lb Energy 3920kcal/16,737kJ; Protein 22.6g; Carbohydrate 1014.4g, of which sugars 1012.2g; Fat 3.3g, of which saturates 0g; Cholesterol 0mg; Calcium 599mg; Fibre 33.7g; Sodium 12139mg.

Apple and sultana chutney

The chutney is perfect served with farmhouse cheese and freshly made soda bread.

Makes about 900g/2lb
350g/12oz cooking apples
115g/4oz/⅔ cup sultanas (golden raisins)
50g/2oz onion
25g/1oz/¼ cup almonds, blanched
5ml/1 tsp white peppercorns
2.5ml/½ tsp coriander seeds
175g/6oz/scant 1 cup sugar
10ml/2 tsp salt
5ml/1 tsp ground ginger
450ml/¾ pint/scant 2 cups cider vinegar
1.5ml/¼ tsp cayenne pepper
red chillies (optional)

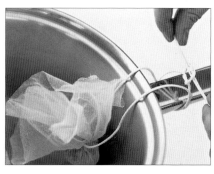

1 Peel, core and chop the apples. Chop the sultanas, onion and almonds. Tie the peppercorns and coriander seeds in muslin (cheesecloth), using a long piece of string, and then tie to the handle of a preserving pan or stainless steel pan.

2 Put the sugar, salt, ground ginger and cider vinegar into the pan, with the cayenne pepper to taste. Heat gently, stirring, until the sugar has completely dissolved.

3 Add the chopped apples, sultanas, onion and almonds. Bring to the boil and simmer for 1½–2 hours, or until most of the liquid has evaporated.

4 Spoon into warmed, sterilized jars and place one chilli in each jar, if using. Leave until cold, then cover, seal and label.

5 Store in a cool dark place. The chutney is best left for a month to mature before use and will keep for at least 6 months, if correctly stored.

Per 900g/2lb Energy 1299kcal/5525kJ; Protein 10.9g; Carbohydrate 299.5g, of which sugars 297.7g; Fat 14.9g, of which saturates 1.1g; Cholesterol 0mg; Calcium 254mg; Fibre 10.4g; Sodium 3.97g.

DRINKS

Apples can be used to make a wide selection of refreshing drinks, both of the alcoholic and the non-alcoholic varieties. For a hot summer's day choose a zingy Apple and Cranberry Spritzer or for a winter warmer a Mulled Cider. For a more substantial refreshment, how about an Apple and Barley Flummery?

Apple and cranberry spritzer

This colourful, zingy cooler combines tangy cranberries with fresh juicy apples and a fragrant hint of vanilla. Top up with sparkling mineral water for a truly refreshing spritzer.

Serves 6–8
6 red eating apples
375g/13oz/3½ cups fresh or frozen
  cranberries, plus extra to decorate
45ml/3 tbsp vanilla syrup
ice cubes
sparkling mineral water

1 Quarter and core the apples then cut the flesh into pieces small enough to fit through a juicer. Push the cranberries and apple chunks through the juicer. Add the vanilla syrup to the juice, cover with clear film (plastic wrap) and chill until ready to serve.

2 Pour the juice into glasses and add one or two ice cubes to each. Top up with sparkling mineral water and decorate with extra cranberries, threaded on to cocktail sticks (toothpicks). Serve immediately.

Per portion Energy 59kcal/255kJ; Protein 0.4g; Carbohydrate 15.3g, of which sugars 15.3g; Fat 0.1g, of which saturates 0g; Cholesterol 0mg; Calcium 6mg; Fibre 2g; Sodium 18mg.

Sweet, sharp shock

The combination of sweet red grape and tart apple is quite delicious. For a longer drink, add sparkling water.

Serves 1
150g/5oz/1¼ cups red grapes
1 red eating apple
1 small cooking apple
crushed ice

1 Slice some grapes and a sliver or two of apple for the decoration. Roughly chop the remaining apples. Push through a juicer with the grapes.

2 Pour over crushed ice, decorate with the sliced fruit and serve immediately.

> **Cook's tip**
> Sugary grapes together with tart apples is one of those perfect flavour combinations that cannot be beaten.

Per portion Energy 156kcal/666kj; Protein 1.2g; Carbohydrate 39.7g, of which sugars 39.7g; Fat 0.3g, of which saturates 0g; Cholesterol 0g; Calcium 25g; Fibre 5.2g; Sodium 7g.

Apple-spiced beer

Lager takes on a whole new dimension in this fun and fruity cooler. Diluted with freshly squeezed apple juice and flavoured with ginger and star anise, it's a great drink for anyone who wants to pace themselves through a party. The spiced apple juice can be made several hours in advance and chilled in a serving jug (pitcher), ready for topping up at the last minute.

Serves 8–10
8 eating apples
25g/1oz fresh root ginger
6 whole star anise
800ml/1⅓ pints/3½ cups lager
crushed ice

1 Quarter and core the apples and, using a small, sharp knife, cut the flesh into pieces small enough to fit through a juicer. Roughly chop the ginger. Push half the apples through the juicer, then juice the ginger and the remaining apples.

2 Put 105ml/7 tbsp of the juice in a small pan with the star anise and heat gently until almost boiling. Add to the remaining juice in a large jug (pitcher) and chill for at least 1 hour.

3 Add the lager to the juice and stir gently to help disperse the froth. Pour over crushed ice in tall glasses and serve immediately.

Per portion Energy 42kcal/178kJ; Protein 0.4g; Carbohydrate 4.8g, of which sugars 4.8g; Fat 0.1g, of which saturates 0g; Cholesterol 0mg; Calcium 6mg; Fibre 0.9g; Sodium 7mg.

Strawberry apple slush

Sweet, juicy strawberries make a delicately fragrant juice. The addition of fresh apple juice and just a hint of vanilla creates a tantalizing treat that's perfect for sipping on a long, lazy summer's afternoon.

Serves 2
300g/11oz/2¾ cups ripe strawberries
2 small, crisp eating apples
10ml/2 tsp vanilla syrup
crushed ice

1 Put aside a couple of the strawberries and hull the remaining ones. Roughly chop the apples. Push all the fruits through a juicer and then stir in the vanilla syrup.

2 Half-fill two tall glasses with crushed ice. Pour over the juice, decorate with the reserved strawberries (slicing them if you like) and serve immediately.

Per portion Energy 95kcal/400kJ; Protein 2g; Carbohydrate 23g, of which sugars 23g; Fat 0g, of which saturates 0g; Cholesterol 0mg; Calcium 28mg; Fibre 3.5g; Sodium 100mg.

Apple and barley flummery

The Celtic countries share this old recipe, which is usually a cooked cold sweet based on oatmeal. This Irish variation is based on barley and also includes apples; sago or tapioca could replace the barley.

Serves 4–6
90ml/6 tbsp pearl barley
675g/1½lb cooking apples, such as
  Bramley's Seedling
50g/2oz/¼ cup caster (superfine) sugar
juice of 1 lemon
45–60ml/3–4 tbsp double (heavy) cream

1 Put 1 litre/1¾ pints/4 cups of water into a pan. Add the barley and bring gently to the boil.

2 Peel, core and slice the apples. Add them to the pan and continue cooking gently until the barley is soft and the apples are cooked.

3 Liquidize the mixture, or press through a sieve (strainer), and return to the rinsed pan. Add the sugar and lemon juice and bring back to the boil.

4 Remove from the heat and allow to cool. Pour into individual glasses, and chill until required. Stir in the cream and serve cold.

Per portion Energy 245kcal/1040kJ; Protein 2.5g; Carbohydrate 47.1g, of which sugars 28.3g; Fat 6.6g, of which saturates 3.8g; Cholesterol 15mg; Calcium 24mg; Fibre 2.7g; Sodium 7mg.

Cranberry and apple punch

This fruit punch is prepared in a slow cooker which extracts maximum flavour from the ginger and lime peel.

Serves 6
1 lime
5cm/2in piece of fresh root ginger,
  peeled and thinly sliced
50g/2oz/¼ cup caster (superfine) sugar
200ml/7fl oz/scant 1 cup near-boiling
  water
475ml/16fl oz/2 cups cranberry juice
475ml/16fl oz/2 cups clear apple juice
ice and chilled sparkling mineral water
  or soda water, to serve (optional)

1 Pare the rind off the lime and place in the slow cooker pot with the ginger and sugar. Pour over the water and stir until the sugar dissolves. Cover and heat on high or auto for 1 hour, then reduce the temperature to low or leave on auto and heat for a further 2 hours. Switch off the slow cooker and leave the syrup to cool completely.

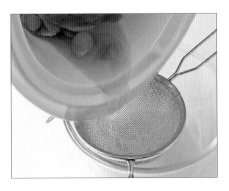

2 Strain the syrup through a fine sieve (strainer) into a punch bowl and discard the ginger and lime rind. Squeeze the juice from the lime and strain through a sieve into the syrup. Stir in the cranberry and apple juices. Cover and chill in the refrigerator for 3 hours.

3 Ladle the punch over ice in tall glasses and top up with water if using.

Per portion: Energy 111kcal/475kJ; Protein 0.1g; Carbohydrate 27.9g, of which sugars 16.5g; Fat 0.1g, of which saturates 0g; Cholesterol 0mg; Calcium 8mg; Fibre 0g; Sodium 2mg.

Drivers' special

For best results when making this bubbly non-alcoholic cocktail always try to use the cloudy natural pressed varieties of apple juice.

Serves 10
1.2 litres/2 pints/5 cups unsweetened
    apple juice
juice of 1 lemon
4 small red eating apples
1.2 litres/2 pints/5 cups ginger beer
ice cubes, to serve
lemon slices or mint sprigs, to decorate

1 Mix the apple juice and lemon juice in a large glass jug (pitcher).

2 Wash and core the apples, but do not peel them. Slice thinly and add the slices to the jug. Stir well and, to prevent browning, check that all the slices are immersed.

3 Cover and set aside in the refrigerator to chill until required.

4 Shortly before serving, add some ice cubes and the ginger beer to the jug, and decorate with lemon slices, or sprigs of mint. Serve in tall glasses.

Per portion Energy 82kcal/352kJ; Protein 0.2g; Carbohydrate 21.4g, of which sugars 21.4g; Fat 0.2g, of which saturates 0g; Cholesterol 0mg; Calcium 15mg; Fibre 0.4g; Sodium 11mg.

Mulled cider

This hot cider cup is easy to make and traditional at Halloween, but it makes a good and inexpensive warming brew for any winter gathering.

Serves 20
2 lemons
1 litre/1¾ pints/4 cups apple juice
2 litres/3½ pints/9 cups medium
    sweet (hard) cider
3 small cinnamon sticks
4–6 whole cloves
slices of lemon, to serve (optional)

1 Wash the lemons and pare the rinds with a vegetable peeler. Blend all the ingredients together in a large stainless steel pan.

2 Set over a low heat and heat the mixture through to infuse (steep) for 15 minutes; do not allow it to boil.

3 Strain the liquid and serve with extra slices of lemon, if you like.

Per portion Energy 61kcal/258kJ; Protein 0.1g; Carbohydrate 9.3g, of which sugars 9.3g; Fat 0.1g, of which saturates 0g; Cholesterol 0mg; Calcium 12mg; Fibre 0g; Sodium 8mg.

INDEX